JAMESTOWN EDUCATION

SIGNATURE READING

LEVEL
G

Mc Graw Hill **Glencoe**

New York, New York   Columbus, Ohio   Chicago, Illinois   Peoria, Illinois   Woodland Hills, California

Reviewers

Marsha Miller, Ed.D
Reading Specialist
Elgin High School
1200 Maroon Drive
Elgin, IL 60120

Kati Pearson
Orange County Public Schools
Literacy Coordinator
Carver Middle School
4500 West Columbia Street
Orlando, FL 32811

Lynda Pearson
Assistant Principal
Reading Specialist
Lied Middle School
5350 Tropical Parkway
Las Vegas, NV 89130

Suzanne Zweig
Reading Specialist/Consultant
Sullivan High School
6631 N. Bosworth
Chicago, IL 60626

Cover Image: Donald E. Carroll/Getty Images

Mc Graw Hill **Glencoe**

The *McGraw·Hill* Companies

ISBN: 0-07-861722-7 (Pupil's Edition)
ISBN: 0-07-861723-5 (Annotated Teacher's Edition)

Send all queries to:
Glencoe/McGraw-Hill
8787 Orion Place
Columbus, OH 43240-4027

3 4 5 6 7 8 9 13 09 08 07 06 05

Contents

How to Use This Book

Working Through the Lessons

The following descriptions will help you work your way through the lessons in this book.

Building Background will help you get ready to read. In this section you might begin a chart, discuss a question, or learn more about the topic of the selection.

Vocabulary Builder will help you start thinking about—and using—the selection vocabulary. You might draw a diagram and label it with vocabulary words, make a word map, match vocabulary words to their synonyms or antonyms, or use the words to predict what might happen in the selection.

Strategy Builder will introduce you to the strategy that you will use to read the selection. First you will read a definition of the strategy. Then you will see an example of how to use it. Often, you will be given ways to better organize or visualize what you will be reading.

Strategy Break will appear within the reading selection. It will show you how to apply the strategy you just learned to the first part of the selection.

Strategy Follow-up will ask you to apply the same strategy to the second part of the selection. Most of the time, you will work on your own to complete this section. Sometimes, however, you might work with a partner or a group of classmates.

Personal Checklist questions will ask you to rate how well you did in the lesson. When you finish totaling your score, you will enter it on the graphs on page 211.

Vocabulary Check will follow up on the work you did in the Vocabulary Builder. After you total your score, you will enter it on page 211.

Strategy Check will follow up on the strategy work that you did in the lesson. After you total your score, you will enter it on page 211.

Comprehension Check will check your understanding of the selection. After you total your score, you will enter it on page 211.

Extending will give ideas for activities that are related to the selection. Some activities will help you learn more about the topic of the selection. Others might ask you to respond to the selection by dramatizing, writing, or drawing something.

Resources such as books, recordings, videos, and Web sites will help you complete the Extending activities.

Graphing Your Progress

The information and graphs on pages 210–211 will help you track your progress as you work through this book. **Graph 1** will help you record your scores for the Personal Checklist and the Vocabulary, Strategy, and Comprehension Checks. **Graph 2** will help you track your overall progress across the book. You'll be able to see your areas of strength, as well as any areas that could use improvement. You and your teacher can discuss ways to work on those areas.

LESSON ❶ Just One of the Guys

Building Background

In the story you're about to read, the characters are all members of a sports team. Think about a time when you were part of a team—either playing sports or working with others on a project. Then get together with a partner and talk about your experiences—both good and bad—as a team member. Make a list of *dos* and *don'ts* for team players, and record your ideas on a separate sheet of paper. For example, under *dos,* you might write: Respect your teammates. Under *don'ts,* you might write: Don't always try to be the star.

breakaway

defenseman

forward

goalie

penalty killing

puck

rink

scrimmage

slap shot

Vocabulary Builder

1. Many of the words in "Just One of the Guys" are related to hockey. Words that are related to a particular topic are called **specialized vocabulary**. The terms in the margin are some of the specialized vocabulary from the selection.

2. Draw a line from each term that you know in Column 1 to its definition in Column 2. Then, as you read the selection, use context clues to figure out any of the terms you aren't familiar with. Go back and match those vocabulary words with their definitions. Double-check your earlier work, too, and make any necessary changes.

COLUMN 1	COLUMN 2
breakaway	area where hockey is played
defenseman	player who guards the goal
forward	player who tries to score
goalie	player who tries to prevent others from scoring
penalty killing	fast-moving shot
puck	practice game
rink	quick move away from opponents
scrimmage	use up time while team member is in penalty box
slap shot	hard rubber disk

3. Save your work. You will use it again in the Vocabulary Check.

Strategy Builder

Identifying Story Elements

- "Just One of the Guys" is a short story. A **short story** tells a sequence of events with a beginning, a middle, and an end. The events in a short story are made up but are often based on events that could happen in real life.

- All stories contain a **setting**, **characters**, and a sequence of events, or **plot**. You will use a story map to help you keep track of these elements in "Just One of the Guys." Study the following story map. It lists and defines the elements that you should be looking for.

Title: (the name of the story)

Setting: (when and where the story takes place)

Main Characters: (the people or animals who perform most of the action)

Problem: (the puzzle or issue that the main characters must try to solve)

Events: (what happens in the story—what the characters do to try to solve the problem)

Solution: (the ending, or conclusion, of the story—how the characters finally solve the problem)

Just One of the Guys

By Donna Gamache

As you read the first part of this story, apply the strategies that you just learned. Try to identify the characters, events, and other elements in the story. You may want to underline them as you read.

I met Tommy and Brent at the door of the **rink** as I was going in for the first hockey practice of the season. Brent ignored me and went on ahead, but Tommy stopped. "Hi, Deena," he said. "You're playing again, eh?"

"Yeah," I told him. "But Mom says I've got to change in the women's washroom this year. Tell the coach I'll be out in a little while."

"O.K.," Tommy said and hurried after Brent, down beneath the stands, while I went on upstairs. I dumped my bag on the floor of the washroom and started pulling out my equipment.

I'd been playing hockey for three years—this would be my fourth—ever since I was nine. But I was still the only girl on the team. All the other girls my age either took figure skating or swimming or dancing. That didn't bother me; I'd always just been "one of the guys" anyway. I hoped that wouldn't change. I had been dressing in the small equipment room inside the boys' locker room, and now I'd miss the fun of getting ready with the rest of the team. But Mom insisted I needed more privacy.

I put on all my equipment and skates, then used the blade protectors to walk downstairs to ice level. The rest of the team—we were the Eagles— were just coming out.

"What's with you, Deena?" asked Brent. "Too good for the rest of us?" He was the only one over the years who had never let me forget that I was a girl playing what was usually a boys' game.

I just ignored him now and started my warm-up exercises. I'd grown a whole lot over the last six months, and most of the guys—including Brent—were shorter than I was. Coach Bingham took one look at my height and suggested I try defense, where the bigger kids usually played. Other years I'd played **forward**, while Brent and Tommy were defensemen, but I heard the coach tell both of them to try out on the forward line.

 Stop here for the Strategy Break.

Strategy Break

If you stopped to create a story map for what you've read so far, it might look like this:

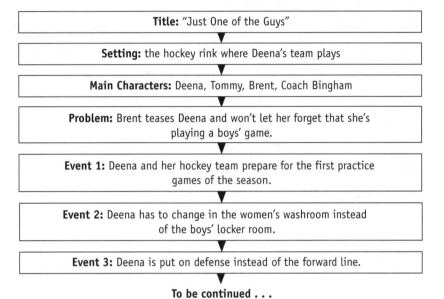

Title: "Just One of the Guys"

Setting: the hockey rink where Deena's team plays

Main Characters: Deena, Tommy, Brent, Coach Bingham

Problem: Brent teases Deena and won't let her forget that she's playing a boys' game.

Event 1: Deena and her hockey team prepare for the first practice games of the season.

Event 2: Deena has to change in the women's washroom instead of the boys' locker room.

Event 3: Deena is put on defense instead of the forward line.

To be continued . . .

Continue looking for story elements as you read the rest of "Just One of the Guys." When you finish reading, you will complete the story map.

 Go on reading to see what happens.

It felt good to be back on skates. The coach had us work on stickhandling drills and a lot of plain hard skating to get our legs in shape. Finally we had a **scrimmage** game, and he paired me on defense with Jibs, who was tall and heavy.

When practice ended, I slipped on my skate protectors and headed upstairs to change. "Can't stand our company, eh?" Brent called, but nobody else said anything.

The next few practices went the same way. Coach Bingham worked us hard and tried us in various combinations. Some days I was paired with Jibs, sometimes with one of the other guys, but always on defense. Tommy and Brent stayed as forwards, and Brent wasn't happy.

"Couldn't I play on defense?" I heard him ask the coach. "I'm used to it, and I'm not that much smaller than Deena." But Coach Bingham shook his head.

After three weeks we were ready for the season opener. I got to the rink in good time, dressed upstairs as usual, then went down and knocked on the locker room door.

"Come downstairs after everyone's dressed," Coach Bingham had suggested. "I'd like you there for the pep talk and any last-minute coaching."

"We're waiting. How come you're so special?" Brent said sarcastically as I went in, but only loud enough for Tommy and me to hear.

"Don't listen to him," Tommy whispered. "He's mad because the coach is putting you on the starting line and not him."

Brent's face turned really red, and he pulled on his hockey mask to cover it. When the coach called my name for **penalty killing**, too, Brent snorted.

"He's just jealous," Tommy said as we trooped out onto the ice. "Don't let it bother you." But it did, a little.

The game started, and it was a close one. We were playing the Pythons, and by the first intermission, there was still no score.

"I need some goals from you forwards," Coach Bingham said as we took a break. "The defense is playing well; keep it up. But forwards, get a hustle on."

The second period started off with a bang. After thirty seconds the Pythons scored—against my line—but right afterward Jibs got the puck up to Tommy, who banged in a goal for us. After one minute we were even again!

"Way to go, Tommy!" I shouted.

The tie lasted until halfway through the third period. Then Jibs and I together got a **breakaway**, and we were both up the ice, passing our forwards and theirs. We moved in on the Python defense. I tried to slip the **puck** across to Jibs, but a Python **defenseman** nabbed it. Before I could stop him, he was away down the ice with no one between him and our **goalie**. He flipped the puck into the corner of our net, and my stomach sank as Coach Bingham signaled us off.

"Don't you remember what the coach said?" Brent snarled as I skated past him. "If one defenseman has a breakaway, the other always stays back. Never *ever* are both defensemen in the other team's end. Don't you listen?"

"I just forgot," I muttered.

"I'll talk to you two later," Coach Bingham said as Jibs and I slumped down on the bench. I felt miserable. That goal had been our fault. Maybe I'd been too distracted by Brent's teasing in the locker room—if only I'd listened more carefully!

It didn't help any when Brent skated back to talk to the coach. "How about putting me on defense?" he asked. "I wouldn't make that mistake."

"We'll stick with what we've practiced for now," Coach Bingham said, and motioned Brent back to center ice.

The rest of the third period sped by. Since we had only four defensemen, the coach couldn't very well bench us, and I was glad to get back on the ice again. I played as hard as I could, and right near the end of the game, it paid off. Jibs got the puck across to me, and I slipped it across to Brent, who snapped in a **slap shot** from the Pythons' blue line.

"Good work, team!" the coach yelled, and Brent actually smiled when I pounded him on the back. The game ended a minute later in a tie.

"Deena!" Coach Bingham called a few minutes later as I started to head upstairs. "You come into the locker room for a few minutes before you change. I want to talk to the *whole* team."

"Yes, sir," I mumbled. I knew he hadn't forgotten our big mistake. I felt as if I had the weight of the rink on my shoulders.

Everyone clumped in and sat down on the benches. Tommy made room for me beside him, and Brent was on my other side.

The coach cleared his throat. "It was a good game, gang," he said. "You played well, and that's what counts. There were a couple of bad mistakes— but the people who made them know it, so I won't harp on them." He paused for a moment, then went on. "There is one thing, though. We're a *team*, don't forget. I want a little more team spirit here. No in-team fighting or criticizing, even when mistakes are made. Understood?"

"Sure, coach," everyone chorused, including Brent.

I stood up to go, and Brent stood up, too, his face red again. "Sorry, Deena," he said quietly. "You're O.K. on defense."

"And you're O.K. on forward," I said. "That was a great goal you scored."

Brent shrugged and looked embarrassed. "It was nice to score," he said. "Maybe I'll get to really like playing forward, once I catch on to it."

I grinned at him as I headed back out of the locker room. Maybe this year would work out, after all. Maybe I could still be "one of the guys." ●

Strategy Follow-up

Now complete the story map for "Just One of the Guys." Begin with Event 4. Parts of the items have been filled in for you.

Title: "Just One of the Guys"

▼

Problem: Brent teases Deena and won't let her forget that she's playing a boys' game.

▼

Event 4: For the season's opening game, Deena

▼

Event 5: Halfway through the third period,

▼

Event 6: Deena makes a mistake, and

▼

Event 7: After Deena passes the puck to Brent,

▼

Event 8: Brent tells Deena that

▼

Solution: When Brent scores a goal after Deena passes the puck to him,

✓Personal Checklist

Read each question and put a check (✓) in the correct box.

1. How well do you understand why Brent treats Deena the way he does at the beginning of the story?
   - ☐ 3 (extremely well)
   - ☐ 2 (fairly well)
   - ☐ 1 (not well)

2. How well did your own experiences and the list of *dos* and *don'ts* you created in Building Background help you understand the problem in this selection?
   - ☐ 3 (extremely well)
   - ☐ 2 (fairly well)
   - ☐ 1 (not well)

3. How well do you understand why Brent's attitude toward Deena changes?
   - ☐ 3 (extremely well)
   - ☐ 2 (fairly well)
   - ☐ 1 (not well)

4. In the Vocabulary Builder, how many specialized vocabulary words were you able to match with their definitions?
   - ☐ 3 (7–9 words)
   - ☐ 2 (4–6 words)
   - ☐ 1 (0–3 words)

5. How well were you able to complete the story map in the Strategy Follow-up?
   - ☐ 3 (extremely well)
   - ☐ 2 (fairly well)
   - ☐ 1 (not well)

Vocabulary Check

Look back at the work you did in the Vocabulary Builder. Then answer each question by circling the correct letter.

1. What is the best definition for *forward*?
   a. player who tries to score
   b. player who tries to prevent others from scoring
   c. player who guards the goal

2. Which vocabulary word means "quick move away from opponents"?
   a. slap shot
   b. scrimmage
   c. breakaway

3. Which vocabulary word means "hard rubber disk"?
   a. puck
   b. rink
   c. slap shot

4. Which definition would you match with *penalty killing*?
   a. area where hockey is played
   b. quick move away from opponents
   c. use up time while team member is in penalty box

5. Which player guards the goal?
   a. goalie
   b. forward
   c. defenseman

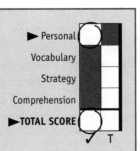

Add the numbers that you just checked to get your total score. (For example, if you checked 3, 2, 3, 2, and 1, your total score would be 11.) Fill in your score here. Then turn to page 211 and transfer your score onto Graph 1.

► Personal
Vocabulary
Strategy
Comprehension
►TOTAL SCORE

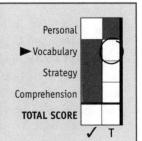

Check your answers with your teacher. Give yourself 1 point for each correct answer, and fill in your Vocabulary score here. Then turn to page 211 and transfer your score onto Graph 1.

Personal
► Vocabulary
Strategy
Comprehension
TOTAL SCORE

Strategy Check

Review the story map that you worked on in the Strategy Follow-up. Also review the selection if necessary. Then answer these questions:

1. Who is *not* a main character in "Just One of the Guys"?
   a. Tommy
   b. Brent
   c. Jibs

2. What could you have written about Deena in Event 4?
   a. She passes the puck to Brent.
   b. She's put on the starting line.
   c. She allows the other team to score.

3. What could you have written about the game halfway through the third period?
   a. Brent scores the tying goal.
   b. Coach Bingham tells the team that they need some goals.
   c. The teams are tied.

4. What does Brent say to Deena after the game?
   a. She is O.K. on defense.
   b. He should play defense.
   c. She should listen more carefully to Coach Bingham.

5. What is the solution to this story's problem?
   a. Brent realizes the importance of playing together as a team.
   b. Deena quits the team.
   c. Coach Bingham lets Brent play defense.

Comprehension Check

Review the story if necessary. Then answer these questions:

1. Why does Brent ignore Deena when they meet at the rink?
   a. Brent doesn't see Deena.
   b. Brent doesn't accept Deena as a teammate.
   c. Brent doesn't want Deena to know that he likes her.

2. Why does Deena change in the women's washroom this year?
   a. because her mother said she needs privacy
   b. because Coach Bingham won't allow her in the boys' locker room
   c. because the girls' locker room is closed for repairs

3. Why is Brent jealous of Deena?
   a. because she's bigger than he is
   b. because the coach puts her on the starting line
   c. because she's a better player than he is

4. What does Brent do after the other team nabs Deena's pass and scores a goal?
   a. He pounds Deena on the back.
   b. He tells Deena that she's a good defender.
   c. He criticizes Deena.

5. Why do you think Brent finally says something nice to Deena after the game?
   a. because Coach Bingham yelled at him
   b. because her teamwork helped him score a goal
   c. because he feels sorry for her

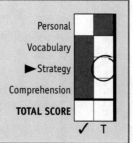

Check your answers with your teacher. Give yourself 1 point for each correct answer, and fill in your Strategy score here. Then turn to page 211 and transfer your score onto Graph 1.

Personal
Vocabulary
▶ Strategy
Comprehension
TOTAL SCORE
✓ T

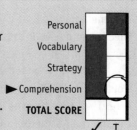

Check your answers with your teacher. Give yourself 1 point for each correct answer, and fill in your Comprehension score here. Then turn to page 211 and transfer your score onto Graph 1.

Personal
Vocabulary
Strategy
▶ Comprehension
TOTAL SCORE
✓ T

Extending

Choose one or more of these activities:

TELL BRENT'S STORY

Imagine that you are Brent. Write a journal entry describing how you feel after the first day of practice. Review the story for clues about Brent's thoughts and feelings.

WRITE A SPORTS REPORT

Be a reporter. First, decide whether you are a newspaper sportswriter or a television sports reporter. Then write a report describing the Eagles' season opener. If you write a newspaper story, be sure to include an attention-grabbing headline. If your story is for the TV news, videotape it or present it to the class.

MAKE A TRADING CARD

Use cardboard or construction paper to create a trading card for one of the hockey players in the story or for the player of your choice. You can learn about real hockey players by exploring one of the resources listed on this page.

Resources

Books

Duplacey, James. *Amazing Forwards.* Hockey Superstars. Beech Tree Books, 1996.

MacGregor, Roy. *The Screech Owls' Home Loss.* The Screech Owls Series. Seal/McClelland, 1998.

Mulford, Philippa Greene. *Emily Smiley Takes a Shot.* Emily Smiley. Tor Books, 1998.

Packard, Edward. *Fire on Ice #181.* Bt Bound, 1999.

Sullivan, George. *All About Hockey.* Putnam Juvenile, 1998.

Web Site

http://www.nhlpa.com/
Read about National Hockey League players on this Web site.

Videos/DVDs

1998 Winter Olympics Hockey Highlights. Twentieth-Century Fox, 1998.

Ice Hockey for Kids. Tapeworm, 1999.

Charlie Johnson

Building Background

Ben Evans, the main character in "Charlie Johnson," is the new kid in town. Think about a time when you experienced a new situation. Maybe you moved to a new neighborhood, entered a new school, or joined a new team. How did you fit in with the new group? What did you do to make friends? Write about your experiences on a separate sheet of paper. As you read "Charlie Johnson," compare your experiences with those of Ben Evans.

bent my ear

call it even

caught me off balance

lend a hand

packed it in

pulled one over

wearing thin

Vocabulary Builder

1. The words in the margin are idioms from "Charlie Johnson." An **idiom** is an expression that has a different meaning from the meanings of its individual words.

2. As you read the story, look for each idiom. Use context clues to figure out its meaning. Then match the meaning with one of the boldfaced phrases below, and write the idiom beside the phrase. The first item has been done for you.

3. Save your work. You will use it again in the Vocabulary Check.

    a. Their excuses are **becoming harder to believe**.   ___wearing thin___

    b. When we paint the room, he can **help**.   _____

    c. After working nonstop for hours, he finally **stopped**.   _____

    d. The old man **talked to me for hours**.   _____

    e. The magician really **fooled us with that trick**.   _____

    f. Do me this favor and we can **say that we don't owe each other anything**.   _____

    g. Her anger really **surprised me**.   _____

Strategy Builder

Drawing Conclusions About Characters

- A **conclusion** is a decision that you reach after thinking about certain facts or information. When you read a story, you often draw conclusions based on information that the author gives you about the characters, setting, or events.

- You can draw conclusions about the **characters,** or people, in a story by paying attention to what they say, do, think, and feel.

- In many stories, the characters change in some way. As you read the paragraphs below, notice how Oscar changes. See if you can draw conclusions about Oscar based on what he says and does.

> "Look, Oscar," said his mother, "a Frisbee contest." She showed her son the flyer. "Why don't you and Popcorn enter it?"
>
> Oscar shook his head. "Who's got time?" he replied. The boy looked down at his dog. "You understand, don't you, Popcorn?" Oscar patted the dog and left for school.
>
> Later, when Oscar came home, Popcorn was waiting. The dog held the Frisbee in its mouth. "Not now," said Oscar, "maybe later." He opened his backpack and started in on his homework. While he was doing a particularly hard math problem, the Frisbee landed on his desk. "Oh, all right," Oscar said to Popcorn. "I'll play with you."
>
> Oscar went outside and began throwing the Frisbee to Popcorn. He laughed and cheered when the dog leapt to catch the toy in its mouth. After an hour of play, they both laid down on the grass, tired but happy. "Maybe I will enter that contest," thought Oscar.

- If you wanted to track the changes in Oscar's character, you could record them on a **character wheel** like the one below. Notice the conclusions that one reader drew about Oscar. They are in *italics*.

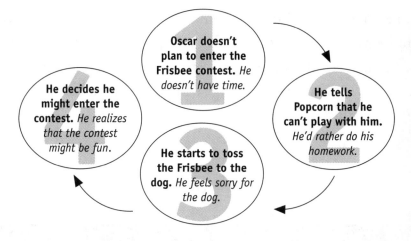

Charlie Johnson

By Joe Smith

As you read the first part of this story, notice what Ben Evans says, does, thinks, and feels. What conclusions can you draw about him?

It was almost four months since we had moved from Boston to this stupid little hick town, and the aura of being the new kid was **wearing thin**. I had to do something soon to make my reputation.

Dave Johnson was the perfect target. He was a big dumb farmer whose place was just down the road from our house. The kids said that he had a temper to match his size, and they were all scared stiff of him. I figured that if I **pulled one over** on Johnson, I'd really be somebody.

I put my plan into effect one December afternoon after school. Mom and Dad weren't home, as usual, so I grabbed a saw out of the cellar and headed down the path behind our house. A short distance through the woods there was a stone wall, then a field full of Christmas trees. Johnson's Christmas trees.

It was almost too easy. I jumped over the wall into the rows of trees and chose a likely victim. As I sawed, I thought about what I was going to tell the kids at school the next day. But as soon as I had the tree cut, a shadow fell over me. I looked up to find the giant farmer standing there. Without a word he hauled me off to his truck and drove me to the farm. "Wait here," he grunted, then disappeared into the barn.

A moment later a figure emerged, but it wasn't the big farmer. It was an old man, wearing a red-checkered coat and big boots.

He shuffled up to my side of the truck and stared at me with watery eyes that were almost hidden by bushy eyebrows. Then he smiled.

"So you're the tree rustler," he said in a gravelly voice. "Come out here where I can get a good look at you."

I glanced nervously toward the barn, and the man chuckled. "I see you've met my son. Don't worry about him. He gets upset easy, but he'll calm down.

"Why, you're barely thirteen or fourteen," he said as he looked me up and down. "The way Dave was talking, I thought we had a hardened criminal on our hands!"

Then he shoved a huge hand toward me. "My name's Charlie Johnson," he said. "You must be the Evans kid that just moved in down the road."

"Yeah, Ben Evans," I said. His grip was surprisingly strong.

"Well, listen, Ben. We're kind of busy right now. Maybe you could **lend me a hand** for a few minutes."

I had been ready for a lecture, even for some yelling and screaming, but this **caught me off balance**.

I followed the old man around to the back of the truck and accepted the trees he handed to me. Then I followed him to the row of empty stands, where we leaned each of the trees in place.

He talked as we worked. I had never met him before, but somehow he seemed to know all about me, my parents, and my friends.

We soon had the stands full of trees. He grabbed one and shoved it toward me.

"Throw it on the back of the truck and get in. I'll give you a ride home. I figure I almost worked the price of that tree out of you by now."

I had to laugh. Until that moment I hadn't realized what the old man was doing.

"Almost, but not quite," he continued. "If you come back about the middle of April when the new trees come in, I'll get another hour of work out of you, and then we'll **call it even**. How does that sound?"

What could I say? I agreed, and he drove me home.

"What are you going to tell your parents about the tree?" he asked as we pulled into the driveway.

"I doubt they'll even care. I barely see them anyway," I said as I hopped out and grabbed the tree. He frowned when I said that, but he gave me a big smile and a wave as he drove away.

My parents didn't ask, but I told everyone at school that I stole the tree, figuring I might as well get something out of the mess. I think some of the kids even believed me.

 Stop here for the Strategy Break.

Strategy Break

What conclusions can you draw about Ben? How has he changed so far? If you were to begin a character wheel for Ben, it might look like this:

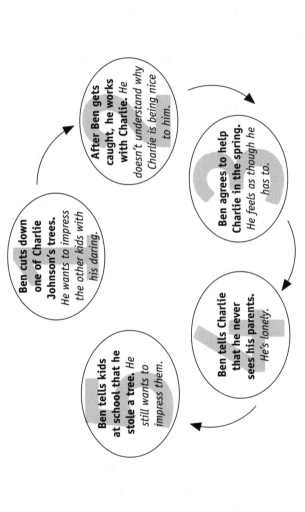

Ben cuts down one of Charlie Johnson's trees. *He wants to impress the other kids with his daring.*

After Ben gets caught, he works with Charlie. *He doesn't understand why Charlie is being nice to him.*

Ben agrees to help Charlie in the spring. *He feels as though he has to.*

Ben tells Charlie that he never sees his parents. *He's lonely.*

Ben tells kids at school that he stole a tree. *He still wants to impress them.*

As you continue reading, keep paying attention to what Ben says, does, thinks, and feels. At the end of the story, you will finish his character wheel. Do you think he'll continue to change?

Go on reading to see what happens.

Winter passed slowly. I had forgotten all about the old man and his trees. He hadn't forgotten about me, though. One spring day I came home to find him sitting in his truck in my driveway.

He brought me to the barn, where there were several long boxes full of seedlings. He showed me the different kinds of trees, and I helped to count and separate them.

When we were done, Charlie told me that if I came back Saturday, he'd pay me to help him plant the trees. I'd never planted a tree in my life and I had better things to do with my Saturday, but a little money would sure impress the other kids, so I said yes.

I showed up early on Saturday. He took me out to the field and showed me what to do. It was hard going, but Charlie kept up a steady stream of talk the whole time.

He had come here when he was younger, too. "Bought this farm and thought I was gonna show the locals how it should be done," he said.

But the '38 hurricane came and blew down his barn and most of the trees on the property. "I would've **packed it in** right there, but the whole town came together and helped me rebuild the barn and get started again. I wasn't such a hotshot after that." He started planting trees to replace what was lost and he'd been at it ever since.

By the end of the day, I was sore all over. The worst part of it was that Charlie had planted twice as many trees as I had and was as fit at the end as when we started.

I spent a lot of time at the farm that summer and earned a bit of money, too. Most times I'd see the younger Johnson, but he'd just scowl and turn away when he saw me. Charlie kept me busy, shearing the trees or mowing the grass between the rows.

I kind of felt sorry for the old man. His son took care of the milk cows and the hayfields, so it seemed as if all he had left were his trees. And the way he **bent my ear**, I figured I must be the only one he had to talk to.

I didn't mind listening, though. I guess I even learned something, and it was funny how he always knew what I'd been up to. I figured that perhaps I was such a celebrity the whole town was talking about me.

That Christmas I bought a tree with my own money. Charlie just laughed, winked, and pocketed the bills. It felt good.

It was a pretty bad winter, and I didn't get over to see him for a couple of months. Then, one gray March morning, my father shoved the morning paper under my nose. There was Charlie's picture on the page. It was a few moments before I figured out that I was looking at the obituaries.

The funeral was a couple of days later. Since I knew he didn't have too many friends, I decided to go so at least someone was there.

The service was held in the church at the center of town. As I walked down the main street I was surprised to see so many cars go by. As I got closer I could see parked cars lining both sides of the street and a policeman directing traffic, but it wasn't until I saw the line before the church door that I realized they were all going the same place I was.

Somewhat in shock, I joined the crowd. When I finally made it inside, all the seats were taken, and I had to stand up against the wall behind the last pew.

I listened as, one after another, people got up to speak. They talked about all Charlie had done for the town and the people in it, how he was always ready to help, but most of all, they talked about how he was their friend.

The minister said a few more words, then the people started rising and filing out of the church. I slipped out and stood looking at the crowd as it grew on the lawn. About an hour before, I was a big shot, going to an old man's funeral out of pity; now I was just a jerk. Embarrassed by my own stupidity, I turned and hurried home.

It was in early April that I found my feet leading me back to the farm. Dave Johnson was in the empty farm stand. He looked up as I approached, that old familiar scowl on his face. "What do you want?" he snarled.

"I thought I could help. With the trees."

He looked annoyed. "Come with me," he said.

He led me into the barn. Three big boxes full of seedlings were on the floor. "It's kind of funny you should show up; they just came this morning." Then he turned and sat on one of them and looked at me.

"I never understood why my father wanted to bother with you," he said, "but I guess he saw something there that I couldn't see. You'd come strutting around here like you were doing him a favor, and I felt like thrashing you. He'd just laugh, though, and he'd say, 'Don't worry, he'll be all right.' I thought he was nuts."

I could have told him to stick it. Maybe a little while ago I would have, but now all I could say was "I'm sorry."

His face softened at that, and I think for a moment he was at a loss for words. "You didn't have to come here," he finally said, "but you did. Maybe Charlie was right after all."

Then he put out his hand, and in the darkness of the barn, I shook it, not because I had anything to prove or because I wanted to impress anyone, but because I just wanted to be his friend. ●

Strategy Follow-up

Work on this activity with a partner or group of classmates. On a large piece of paper, copy the character wheel below. Then complete circles 6–10 with information from the second half of the story.

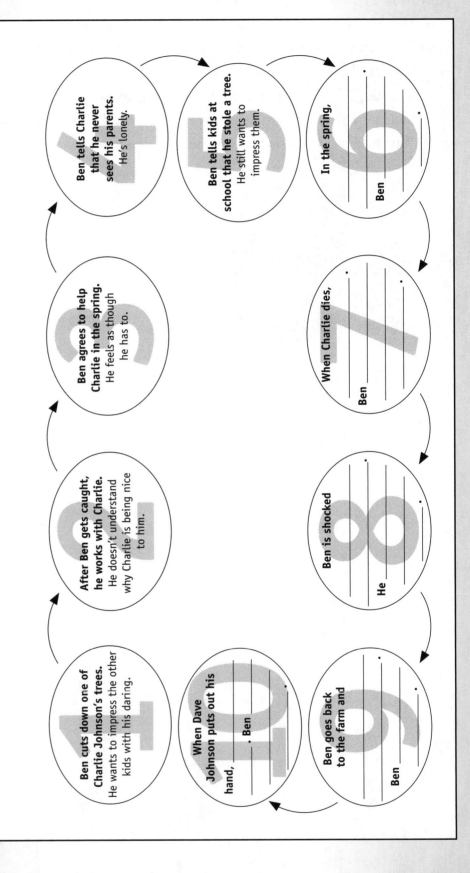

Ben cuts down one of Charlie Johnson's trees. He wants to impress the other kids with his daring.

After Ben gets caught, he works with Charlie. He doesn't understand why Charlie is being nice to him.

Ben agrees to help Charlie in the spring. He feels as though he has to.

Ben tells Charlie that he never sees his parents. He's lonely.

Ben tells kids at school that he stole a tree. He still wants to impress them.

In the spring, Ben

When Charlie dies, Ben

Ben is shocked He

Ben goes back to the farm and Ben

When Dave Johnson puts out his hand, Ben

✓Personal Checklist

Read each question and put a check (✓) in the correct box.

1. How well do you understand what happened in "Charlie Johnson"?
   - ☐ 3 (extremely well)
   - ☐ 2 (fairly well)
   - ☐ 1 (not well)

2. How well were you able to use what you wrote in Building Background to help you understand how Ben felt as the new kid in town?
   - ☐ 3 (extremely well)
   - ☐ 2 (fairly well)
   - ☐ 1 (not well)

3. In the Vocabulary Builder, how many idioms were you able to correctly identify?
   - ☐ (6–7 idioms)
   - ☐ (3–5 idioms)
   - ☐ (0–2 idioms)

4. How well were you able to complete the character wheel in the Strategy Follow-up?
   - ☐ 3 (extremely well)
   - ☐ 2 (fairly well)
   - ☐ 1 (not well)

5. How well do you understand why Ben goes back to the farm after Charlie dies?
   - ☐ 3 (extremely well)
   - ☐ 2 (fairly well)
   - ☐ 1 (not well)

Vocabulary Check

Look back at the work you did in the Vocabulary Builder. Then answer each question by circling the correct letter.

1. Which idiom could you use to replace the phrase "fooled us with that trick"?
   a. bent our ear
   b. pulled one over
   c. caught us off balance

2. What does Ben mean when he says "the aura of being the new kid was wearing thin"?
   a. It was no longer exciting to be known as the new kid.
   b. He was losing weight.
   c. The new kid at school was getting on his nerves.

3. What would a helpful person be most likely to do?
   a. call it even
   b. be caught off balance
   c. lend a hand

4. After the hurricane blew down his barn, Charlie almost "packed it in." In this context, which phrase means the same as *packed it in*?
   a. stopped doing something
   b. filled a suitcase
   c. ate a big meal

5. Ben says that Charlie "bent my ear." In this context, which phrase has the same meaning as that idiom?
   a. twisted his ear
   b. talked and talked
   c. yelled at him

Add the numbers that you just checked to get your Personal Checklist score. Fill in your score here. Then turn to page 211 and transfer your score onto Graph 1.

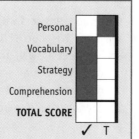

Check your answers with your teacher. Give yourself 1 point for each correct answer, and fill in your Vocabulary score here. Then turn to page 211 and transfer your score onto Graph 1.

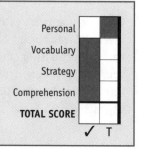

Strategy Check

Review the story and the character wheel that you completed in the Strategy Follow-up. Then answer these questions:

1. What conclusion could you draw when Ben goes back to work for Charlie?
   a. Ben plans to cut down another one of Charlie's trees.
   b. Ben likes working with Charlie.
   c. Ben is angry with Charlie.

2. Why does Ben go to Charlie's funeral?
   a. because he loves Charlie as a friend
   b. because he feels sorry for Charlie
   c. because he wants to be a good friend to Dave

3. Why is Ben surprised to see so many people at the funeral?
   a. He thought that everyone was afraid of Dave.
   b. He didn't think the town was that big.
   c. He thought that Charlie didn't have any friends.

4. Why do you think Ben offers to help Charlie's son, Dave?
   a. He misses Charlie.
   b. He knows Dave needs the help.
   c. He feels sorry for Dave.

5. Why does Ben shake Dave Johnson's hand?
   a. He wants to impress Dave.
   b. He wants Dave to hire him.
   c. He wants to be Dave's friend.

Comprehension Check

Review the story if necessary. Then answer these questions:

1. What does Ben decide to do to make his reputation?
   a. He drives his mother's car to school.
   b. He steals one of Dave Johnson's cows.
   c. He cuts down one of Charlie Johnson's trees.

2. How does Charlie Johnson treat Ben when they meet?
   a. Charlie scolds Ben.
   b. Charlie is friendly and gentle.
   c. Charlie ignores Ben.

3. Why does Charlie take an interest in Ben?
   a. Charlie feels sorry for the boy.
   b. Charlie wants to be paid for the tree that Ben cut down.
   c. Charlie is lonely and friendless.

4. What surprises Ben about Charlie's funeral?
   a. the crowd of people there
   b. the fact that Dave isn't there
   c. the fact that his parents attend the funeral

5. Why do you think Dave Johnson didn't like Ben?
   a. Ben tried to steal a tree.
   b. Ben acted as if he was doing Charlie a favor.
   c. Dave was jealous of Ben.

Check your answers with your teacher. Give yourself 1 point for each correct answer, and fill in your Strategy score here. Then turn to page 211 and transfer your score onto Graph 1.

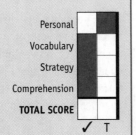

Check your answers with your teacher. Give yourself 1 point for each correct answer, and fill in your Comprehension score here. Then turn to page 211 and transfer your score onto Graph 1.

Extending

Choose one or both of these activities:

DRAW CHARLIE JOHNSON'S PORTRAIT

Draw a portrait of Charlie Johnson. Review the story, and try to include as many details as possible in the portrait. For example, the story mentions a red-checkered coat, big boots, watery eyes, and bushy eyebrows. It also mentions that Charlie has huge hands and that he drives a truck. Share your finished portrait with your classmates.

READ ABOUT FRIENDSHIP

Choose one of the novels listed on this page and read it in your free time. As you read, think about how friendship changes the characters. Then choose a character and create a character wheel to record how he or she changes.

Resources

Books

Anderson, Peggy King, *First Day Blues*. Decision Is Yours. Parenting Press, 1993.

Baker, Camy. *Camy Baker's How to Be Popular in the Sixth Grade*. Camy Baker's Series. Skylark, 1998.

Pfeffer, Susan Beth. *Beth Makes a Friend*. Portraits of Little Women. Delacorte Press, 1998.

Zemser, Amy Bronwen. *Beyond the Mango Tree*. HarperTrophy, 2000.

Web Site

http://www.chunkymonkey.com
This Web site provides easy-to-follow drawing lessons. It also provides a showcase for kids' art.

How Buildings Take Shape

Building Background

In the space below, draw a picture of a building that you see every day. You may choose to draw a picture of a house, an apartment building, or an office building.

Now study your drawing. What shapes did you use? The article you are about to read talks about a shape found in many buildings—the triangle.

applications

architect

collapse

horizontal

rigid

truss

vertical

Vocabulary Builder

1. The words in the margin are **specialized vocabulary** words. Specialized vocabulary words are related to a particular topic. These words all have to do with building.

2. With a partner or on your own, look up each word in a dictionary. Then find the words in the statements below. If a statement is true, write a **T** on the line beside it. If a statement is false, write an **F** on the line.

3. Save your work. You will use it again in the Vocabulary Check.

_____ a. A tool with many **applications** has many uses.

_____ b. Heavy snow caused the roof to **collapse**.

_____ c. **Architects** clean teeth for a living.

_____ d. You are **horizontal** when standing.

_____ e. A **rigid** bar will not bend.

_____ f. A **truss** supports heavy weight.

_____ g. A flagpole looks like a **vertical** line.

Strategy Builder

Following Sequence in an Informational Article

- An **informational article** gives facts and information about a particular subject, or topic. The **topic** of an article is what the article is all about. The topic is often mentioned in the **title** of the article. For example, "How Buildings Take Shape" is about buildings and the shapes used to construct them.

- To help you understand an informational article, the writer organizes it logically. In "How Buildings Take Shape," the writer uses sequence to organize the instructions for two experiments. **Sequence** is the order in which something takes place.

- Sequence helps readers follow instructions of all kinds. Read the instructions for cooking noodles below. Notice that the sequence of steps makes sense.

> Fill a large pot with a gallon of water.
>
> Place the pot on the stove, cover, and bring the water to a boil.
>
> Place the noodles and a tablespoon of salt into the boiling water.
>
> Boil the noodles for 8 minutes, stirring occasionally.
>
> Drain the noodles, and serve immediately.

- Another way to arrange steps is on a **sequence chain**. Notice that the steps appear in the same order as they do in the recipe.

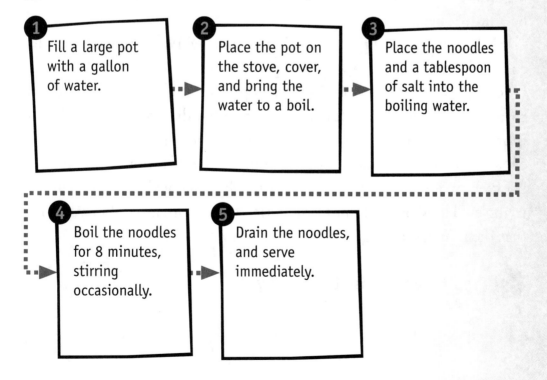

How Buildings Take Shape

by Kim Williams

As you read the first part of this article, try to apply the strategies that you just learned. Notice the sequence of steps the author uses to describe the experiment.

The humble triangle is one of the architect's most important tools.

In ancient times, **architects** used triangles to give buildings shape, and triangles are still used in most buildings.

When many children first learn to draw, they show a house as a square with a triangle on top of it. In fact, the roofs of most houses really are made like triangles. This shape lets rainwater run off.

But triangles are used in roofs for another reason as well. A triangle is a strong shape because it's a **rigid** form. To an architect, that means this form won't **collapse** of its own weight and that it can hold up more weight as well.

Try this experiment. You'll need ten paper clips and five pieces of drinking straws. (Four of the pieces should be the same length. The fifth should be a little longer.)

Hook eight paper clips in pairs. These pairs will be corners. Slide each end of the four short straws onto a paper clip.

You've just made a square. But if you pick up the square by any of its corners, it changes shape. It collapses into a flat diamond shape called a rhombus. You can see that a square is not a rigid form.

Now use two more paper clips to connect the fifth (longer) straw between two opposite corners. This straw has changed the square into two triangles. The shape may not be a perfect square anymore, but you can see that the triangles are rigid.

 Stop here for the Strategy Break.

Strategy Break

If you were to put the steps in the experiment in a sequence chain, they might look like this:

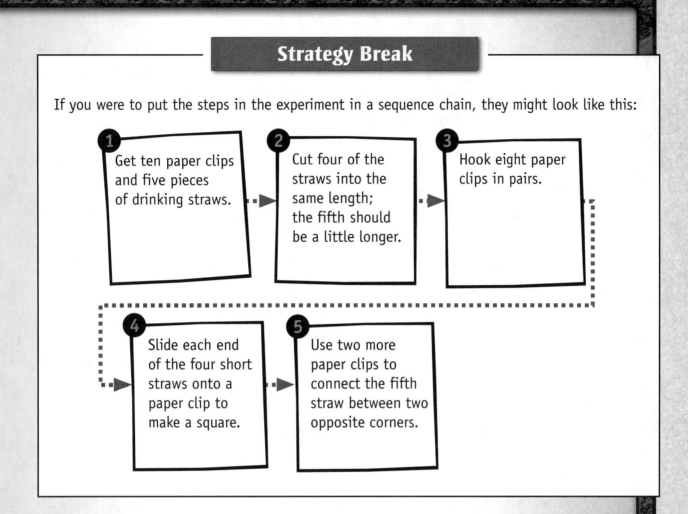

 Go on reading.

Strong Supports

The rigidity of triangles has helped architects solve some big problems. One of these problems is how to support a heavy weight over a large space, such as a bridge over a river or a roof over a wide building like a supermarket.

The architect can try to use a single solid beam of wood or steel, but that will weigh a lot. If it is too long, it will break in the middle from its own weight. Now what is there to do? The solution is a strong kind of beam called a **truss**. A truss is built out of triangles, which give it strength.

Trusses weigh less than solid beams because the open spaces between the sides of the triangles don't weigh anything. And since triangles are rigid shapes, a truss can support many times more weight than a simple beam can. Engineers have discovered many different forms for the truss, but all of them use triangles.

Centuries ago, Greek and Roman architects used wooden trusses to hold roofs made of heavy clay tiles. Today, trusses made of steel are light yet strong. Next time you go to the supermarket or a gymnasium, look up to see whether triangles were used to help hold up the roof.

Building the Pyramids

A remarkable kind of triangle was used in building the great pyramids of Giza in Egypt. That triangle was not part of the pyramids. It was used to draw some of the lines that were needed to guide the work.

Horizontal and **vertical** lines are basic elements in any architectural design. And when a vertical line crosses a horizontal line, they form another important element in architectural plans: the right angle.

People live with right angles every day. When we stand straight, we stand at right angles to the ground. Each corner of each page in this book is a right angle. The walls of buildings meet the floors at right angles. You can see that right angles are important to architects.

In ancient Egypt, architects had to make right angles without the tools that modern architects and builders have. As a guide to help mark out the square bases of the pyramids, they used the simplest of devices: a rope with twelve knots. With this rope, they could make a triangle that always had a right angle at one corner.

Egyptian builders used this triangle to make sure the corners of buildings were neat and square. (A "square" corner has an accurate right angle.) That's why this triangle is sometimes called the Egyptian triangle.

Make one to see how it works. You'll need two pens or markers and a ball of string or yarn. Lay one of the markers next to the string, and mark its length on the string with the other marker. Continue measuring and marking the string until you have marked off twelve equal segments. Next, tie a knot at each point you marked. Finally, cut off the string right after the twelfth knot.

This is your Egyptian tool. To make it work, arrange the string in the shape of a triangle. Make the first side three marker-lengths, the second side four marker-lengths, and the third side five marker-lengths. If you want to keep the string in place, tape it to a piece of cardboard. You will see that the angle between the side measuring three and the side measuring four is exactly a right angle, the angle architects use the most.

At first, the basic shape of the triangle may seem plain and ordinary. But the shape has many **applications** in the art of architecture *because* it's a basic form that is also rigid. To an architect, the triangle's simplicity makes it a thing of beauty. ●

Strategy Follow-up

Now create a sequence chain to show the steps in the second experiment. Parts of the steps have been filled in for you.

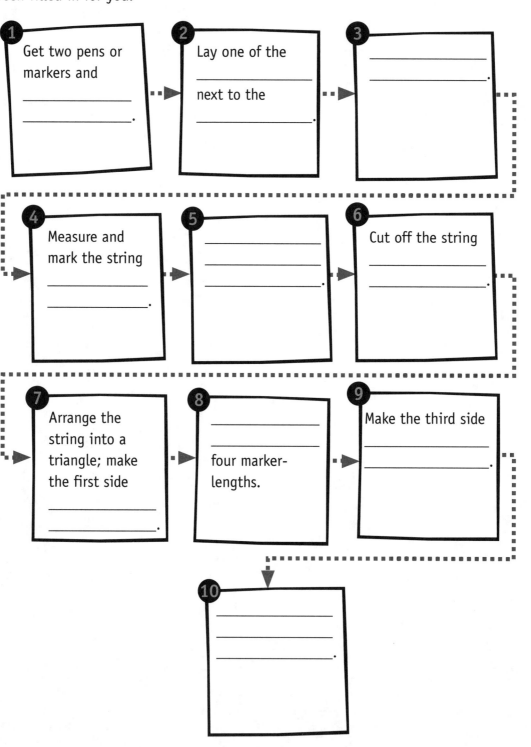

1 Get two pens or markers and _____ _____.

2 Lay one of the _____ next to the _____.

3 _____ _____.

4 Measure and mark the string _____ _____.

5 _____ _____.

6 Cut off the string _____ _____.

7 Arrange the string into a triangle; make the first side _____ _____.

8 _____ _____ four marker-lengths.

9 Make the third side _____ _____.

10 _____ _____ _____.

✓Personal Checklist

Read each question and put a check (✓) in the correct box.

1. How well do you understand the information presented in this article?
   - ☐ 3 (extremely well)
   - ☐ 2 (fairly well)
   - ☐ 1 (not well)

2. How well did the activity in Building Background help you understand how shapes are used to construct buildings?
   - ☐ 3 (extremely well)
   - ☐ 2 (fairly well)
   - ☐ 1 (not well)

3. In the Strategy Follow-up, how well were you able to use a sequence chain to organize the steps in the experiment?
   - ☐ 3 (extremely well)
   - ☐ 2 (fairly well)
   - ☐ 1 (not well)

4. In the Vocabulary Builder, how many of the sentences did you correctly identify as true or false?
   - ☐ 3 (6–7 sentences)
   - ☐ 2 (4–5 sentences)
   - ☐ 1 (0–3 sentences)

5. How well can you explain why triangles are important to architects?
   - ☐ 3 (extremely well)
   - ☐ 2 (fairly well)
   - ☐ 1 (not well)

Vocabulary Check

Look back at the work you did in the Vocabulary Builder. Then answer each question by circling the correct letter.

1. Which other word or phrase has the same meaning as *collapse?*
   a. explode
   b. rise up
   c. cave in

2. Which word could you substitute for *applications?*
   a. layers
   b. uses
   c. coats

3. Which vocabulary word means "upright"?
   a. truss
   b. horizontal
   c. vertical

4. Which vocabulary word is the opposite of *vertical?*
   a. horizontal
   b. rigid
   c. truss

5. Which of the following is *not* something that an architect does?
   a. plans and designs buildings
   b. develops different forms for trusses
   c. cleans teeth

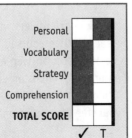

Add the numbers that you just checked to get your Personal Checklist score. Fill in your score here. Then turn to page 211 and transfer your score onto Graph 1.

Personal
Vocabulary
Strategy
Comprehension
TOTAL SCORE
✓ T

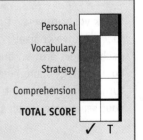

Check your answers with your teacher. Give yourself 1 point for each correct answer, and fill in your Vocabulary score here. Then turn to page 211 and transfer your score onto Graph 1.

Personal
Vocabulary
Strategy
Comprehension
TOTAL SCORE
✓ T

Strategy Check

Review the sequence chain that you completed in the Strategy Follow-up. Then answer these questions:

1. What do you need in order to complete step 1 of the experiment?
   a. markers and straws
   b. markers and pens
   c. markers and a ball of string

2. How many segments should be measured and marked on the string?
   a. twelve
   b. four
   c. five

3. Which step would you do just *before* you cut off the string?
   a. Mark the length of the pen on the string.
   b. Arrange the string into a triangle.
   c. Tie a knot at each marked point.

4. How should you arrange the three sides into a triangle?
   a. Make the first side five marker-lengths. Make the second side three marker-lengths. Make the third side four marker-lengths.
   b. Make the first side three marker-lengths. Make the second side four marker-lengths. Make the third side five marker-lengths.
   c. Make the first side three marker-lengths. Make the second side five marker-lengths. Make the third side four marker-lengths.

5. What is the final step in the experiment?
   a. Cut off the string after the twelfth knot.
   b. Lay a pen next to the string.
   c. Tape the string to a piece of cardboard.

Comprehension Check

Review the selection if necessary. Then answer these questions:

1. Which of the following does *not* explain why triangles are used in roofs?
   a. The shape lets water run off.
   b. A triangle is a strong, rigid shape.
   c. No other shape would look right.

2. What big architectural problem did the triangle help solve?
   a. how to build a bridge over a wide river
   b. how to build stairs
   c. how to build brick walls

3. According to the selection, where might you see trusses?
   a. at the bottom of a swimming pool
   b. in a living or dining room
   c. in a supermarket or gymnasium

4. How did the pyramid builders use triangles?
   a. They used a triangle to draw lines that guided their work.
   b. The stones they used were triangular shaped.
   c. They built triangular roofs on the pyramids.

5. Which important element helps builders design straight walls?
   a. horizontal lines
   b. the right angle
   c. vertical lines

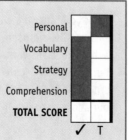

Check your answers with your teacher. Give yourself 1 point for each correct answer, and fill in your Strategy score here. Then turn to page 211 and transfer your score onto Graph 1.

Personal
Vocabulary
Strategy
Comprehension
TOTAL SCORE
✓ T

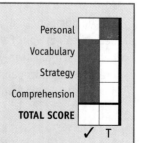

Check your answers with your teacher. Give yourself 1 point for each correct answer, and fill in your Comprehension score here. Then turn to page 211 and transfer your score onto Graph 1.

Personal
Vocabulary
Strategy
Comprehension
TOTAL SCORE
✓ T

Extending

Choose one or more of these activities:

PERFORM THE EXPERIMENTS

Do one or both of the experiments described in this article. Use the sequence chains to help you follow the steps in order. Show your results to a classmate.

MAKE A HOW-TO VIDEO

Make a video demonstrating one of the experiments in this article. Give a brief introduction to explain the importance of the triangle. Then describe the materials needed for the experiment. Finally, perform the steps in sequential order.

RESEARCH THE PYRAMIDS AT GIZA

Work alone or with a group of classmates to find out more about the construction of the pyramids at Giza. Use the resources listed on this page to help you with your research. Then present your findings to your class.

Resources

Books

Macaulay, David. *Pyramid.* Houghton Mifflin/Walter Lorraine, 1982.

Morgan, Sally. *Triangles and Pyramids.* The World of Shapes. Thomson Learning, 1995.

Ross, Catherine Sheldrick. *Triangles: Shapes in Math, Science, and Nature.* Kids Can Press, 1997.

Van Der Meer, Ron, and Deyan Sudjic. *The Architecture Pack: A Unique Three-Dimensional Tour of Architecture over the Centuries; What Architects Do, How They Do It.* Knopf, 1997.

Web Sites

http://www.exploratorium.edu/science_explorer/geo_gumdrops.html
This Web site gives instructions on a simple activity showing several basic principles in architecture.

http://www.pbs.org/wgbh/nova/pyramid
This Web site contains information and pictures related to the pyramids in Egypt.

Video/DVD

This Old Pyramid. Nova. WGBH Boston Video, 1998.

bleak

churning

disastrous

flickered

nor'easter

raged

swirled

whimper

The Lighthouse Keeper's Daughter

CLIPBOARD

bleak
_____

churning
_____

disastrous
_____

flickered
_____

CLIPBOARD

nor'easter
_____

raged
_____

swirled
_____

whimper
_____

Building Background

Abbie, the main character in "The Lighthouse Keeper's Daughter," keeps a log-book in which she records important daily events. She also describes some of her personal thoughts and feelings. On a separate sheet of paper, write a logbook entry about an average day in your life. Describe your daily responsibilities at school and at home. Express your thoughts and feelings about your duties. After you finish reading the story, compare your duties and thoughts with Abbie's. How are they alike? How are they different?

Vocabulary Builder

1. Read the words in the margin. They are from "The Lighthouse Keeper's Daughter."

2. On the clipboards, write a meaning for each word. Look up unfamiliar words in a dictionary. If a word has more than one meaning, predict how it might be used in the story and use that meaning.

3. Then use the vocabulary words and the title to help you predict what might happen in the story. Write your predictions on the lines below. Use as many vocabulary words as possible.

4. Save your work. You will use it again in the Vocabulary Check.

_____

_____

_____

Strategy Builder

Mapping a Story's Plot

- **Historical fiction** tells a made-up story based on real historical events. "The Lighthouse Keeper's Daughter" is historical fiction that describes events that could have happened to lighthouse keepers in the mid-1800s.

- Historical fiction contains the same elements that you would find in any story. These elements include a **setting** (when and where the story takes place), **characters** (the people in the story), and **plot** (the events in the story).

- The plot of a story is driven by a **conflict,** or problem, faced by the main character. The events in the plot show how the character deals with and solves this conflict. As a character deals with the conflict, the rising action of the plot builds to a climax. The **climax** is the turning point of the story—the point at which the problem is settled. The falling action after the climax leads to a **resolution,** or solution of the problem.

- You will use a **story map** to keep track of the plot in "The Lighthouse Keeper's Daughter." Study the following story map. It shows the development of the plot in "Just One of the Guys," the story in Lesson 1.

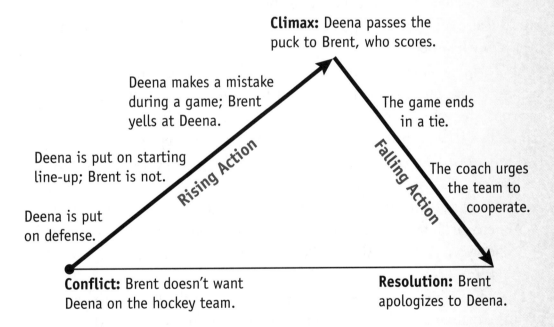

Climax: Deena passes the puck to Brent, who scores.

Deena makes a mistake during a game; Brent yells at Deena.

Deena is put on starting line-up; Brent is not.

Deena is put on defense.

Rising Action

Falling Action

The game ends in a tie.

The coach urges the team to cooperate.

Conflict: Brent doesn't want Deena on the hockey team.

Resolution: Brent apologizes to Deena.

The Lighthouse Keeper's Daughter

By Laura A. Badami

As you read the first part of this story, apply the strategies that you just learned. Try to identify the conflict and some of the events in the plot's rising action.

19 January 1856
Temperature 28°F; Barometer 29.8" & falling
 Papa rowed ashore this morning to collect his pay and buy supplies.
I'm in charge of the towers until he returns tomorrow.
Abigail Burgess

Abbie was 14 years old at the time.

"Abbie, play with me!" Jane called. "I'm bored!"

Abbie laid her pen down and closed the thick logbook. Trouble followed her sister everywhere, and if Abbie didn't entertain her soon, she'd be wailing.

"Catch!" Jane shouted from across the yard and flung a red ball high into the air. When it disappeared over the eaves and didn't come back, she began to **whimper**.

Abbie sighed and squinted into the sky. "It must be stuck on the roof again," she said and stalked off to find the ladder. When she was alone on the roof, she gazed out across Matinicus Rock. "The Rock," as she and Jane called it, was thirty-four acres of **bleak**, wave-swept granite, twenty-two miles off the coast of Maine. Huge boulders, tossed carelessly by the sea during storms, provided the only landscape. Between the twin granite light towers nestled the small dwelling the Burgess family called home.

"When's breakfast?" Jane called from below. "My stomach is starving."

"When you fetch it," Abbie called back. Couldn't that girl do anything for herself?

The wind whipped Abbie's long skirts as she climbed down the ladder with the ball and headed back to the kitchen. After fixing breakfast, she'd have to attend to the lamps in both towers: clean their glass, trim their wicks, fill them with oil. They had to be ready for the evening lighting.

Once inside, Abbie shut out the winter cold and kissed her mother lightly on the cheek. "How are you feeling, Mama?"

The tiny smile on Mama's thin lips disappeared. "The pain's moved into my wrists and fingers."

"I'll get you a warm cloth," Abbie said. She lifted the heavy iron kettle off the stove and poured hot water into a bowl. Then she dipped a clean cloth in it, wrung out the steaming water, and placed the cloth over Mama's hands. "This will ease your pain."

Mama had developed arthritis after Jane was born. Most days she couldn't get out of bed, so Abbie had to take care of the household chores—and of Jane.

The kitchen door flung open. "A storm's coming," Jane said breathlessly.

Abbie peered out at the eastern sky, now flat and leaden. The sea had turned into a gray mass of waves. "A **nor'easter**," she said calmly, but inside, her stomach was **churning**. A nor'easter could last for days, and Papa wouldn't be able to return until it was over. "I'd better get to the lamps. We could be in for a long haul."

30 January 1856

Temperature 25°F; Barometer 29.3" & falling

The nor'easter roared in last week, and after eight days it blows as fiercely as ever. Yesterday, Jane insisted on accompanying me to the southern tower. A giant wave came out of nowhere and almost washed her off the Rock. She'll stay inside from now on.

Abigail Burgess

 Stop here for the Strategy Break.

Strategy Break

If you were to map the plot of "The Lighthouse Keeper's Daughter" so far, your map might look like this:

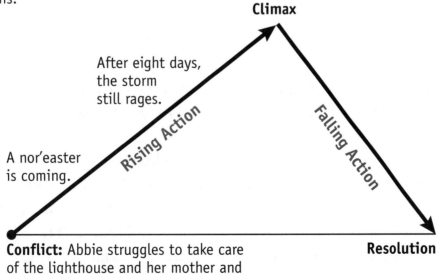

As you continue reading, keep tracking the development of the plot. Pay attention to the events that build toward the climax and lead to the resolution.

Go on reading to see what happens.

"Abbie!" Jane cried. "The floor is leaking!"

Abbie dropped her pen and dashed to the kitchen. Saltwater seeped under the door, spreading rapidly across the stone floor.

"Jane, help me get the rest of the food," Abbie said. "Then I'll need your help with Mama. We ought to stay in the northern tower tonight."

"What about my hens?" Jane cried. "They'll drown if we don't bring them in!"

Abbie glanced out the window. The full fury of the storm was upon them, and massive black waves pounded the Rock. To go out now would be unwise and dangerous. She looked at Jane. The girl's small face was tight with fear for her beloved hens.

"Fetch me the basket," Abbie said. "I'll save your friends." She waited for a break in the rollers, then shoved the kitchen door open against the wicked fury of the wind. Her woolen skirt hung heavy as the icy water **swirled** around her knees. She waded the few yards to the chicken coop and snatched the frightened creatures, who squawked in protest. With her heart pounding wildly, Abbie clutched the basket to her chest and struggled back to the house. Once inside, she bolted the door, leaning against it and gasping for breath.

"Look! Look!" cried Jane from the window. "The sea is coming!"

Abbie dragged herself to Jane and looked out. An enormous wave swept the Rock, splintering the coop and washing away its remains.

"Come, Jane," Abbie said. "We must get Mama and hurry to the tower."

10 February 1856

Temperature 24°F; Barometer 29.6" & steady

Our food is almost gone. The vegetables gave out last night, and we must ration ourselves to only one cup of cornmeal and one egg a day. Though the hens entertain Jane, I admit I've thought of roasting one for dinner.

Abigail Burgess

The yellow light from the lantern **flickered** across the pages of the logbook. Abbie rubbed her eyes. She'd have to check the tower lights shortly.

"Let's play catch," Jane said, bounding up into the lantern's light.

"We can roll the ball across the floor," Abbie said, "but we can't throw it. If it mistakenly bounced into the lantern room, it would be **disastrous**."

Jane stomped her foot loudly on the wooden floor. "I want to play *catch!*"

"No!" Abbie yelled back.

"Abbie!" Mama shouted. "Please keep it down."

Abbie swung around, marched into the lantern room, and stared out the window. Angry black clouds rolled across the sky. That's how I feel, she thought. She was tired of everyone depending on her. She leaned her forehead against the cold glass, fixing her eyes on the storm. A tiny light flickered among the fierce waves.

"A ship," Abbie whispered. Captains relied on the towers to warn them of danger and guide them to safety. They needed her, just like Mama and Jane did. "I'd better get to work," she sighed.

Abbie readied the lamp for another long night, then peeked into the other room. Jane was sitting quietly, listening to Mama sing her a lullaby. Abbie tiptoed into the room and knelt beside her family. It felt warm and safe here while the storm **raged** on outside.

16 February 1856

Temperature 37°F; Barometer 30.0" & rising

For the first day this month, the sun has decided to stretch its rays, and the wind has calmed to a gentle breeze. After four weeks, it seems the storm has passed.

Abbie laid her pen down and opened the kitchen door. She leaned against the frame and breathed in the fresh salty air. The warmth of the sun felt good. The logbook could wait.

"Abbie!" a deep voice shouted. "Thank God you're safe!"

The girl's eyes flew open. "Papa!" She ran and flung herself into his strong arms.

"How are your mother and Jane?" Papa asked.

"They're fine," Abbie said, snuggling deeper into his warm arms.

Papa tightened his hold on his daughter. "I looked every evening for the beams from our lighthouses. They were always there."

"I was scared," Abbie said. "I thought the storm would never end."

Papa tilted Abbie's face up and looked into her eyes. "I was scared, too. But you're a strong girl. And I'm proud of you." ●

Strategy Follow-up

Now continue the story map that you began in the Strategy Break. Parts of the events have been filled in for you.

Climax: The storm passes.

During the storm, Abbie rations
and lights the tower lights for
_____ _____ _____ .

Abbie rescues _____ _____
and takes her mother and sister
_____ _____ .

After eight days, the storm still rages.

A nor'easter is coming.

Rising Action

Conflict: Abbie struggles to take care
of the lighthouse and her mother and
sister while her father is away.

Abbie opens the tower door and breathes
in the fresh air. Then _____
_____ _____ _____
_____ _____ _____
_____ _____ _____ .

Falling Action

Resolution: Abbie's father
comes home and tells her that
_____ _____ _____ .

✓Personal Checklist

Read each question and put a check (✓) in the correct box.

1. How well do you understand why Abbie has so many responsibilities?
    - ☐ 3 (extremely well)
    - ☐ 2 (fairly well)
    - ☐ 1 (not well)

2. How well did Building Background help you compare your responsibilities with Abbie's?
    - ☐ 3 (extremely well)
    - ☐ 2 (fairly well)
    - ☐ 1 (not well)

3. How well do you understand why Abbie feels like the black clouds she sees rolling across the sky?
    - ☐ 3 (extremely well)
    - ☐ 2 (fairly well)
    - ☐ 1 (not well)

4. In the Vocabulary Builder, how many words were you able to use in your prediction?
    - ☐ 3 (6–8 words)
    - ☐ 2 (3–5 words)
    - ☐ 1 (0–2 words)

5. In the Strategy Follow-up, how well were you able to complete the story map?
    - ☐ 3 (extremely well)
    - ☐ 2 (fairly well)
    - ☐ 1 (not well)

Vocabulary Check

Look back at the work you did in the Vocabulary Builder. Then answer each question by circling the correct letter.

1. When Jane's ball disappears, she begins to whimper. What does *whimper* mean?
    - a. cry
    - b. laugh
    - c. talk very loudly

2. Which of the following words best describes "the Rock"?
    - a. churning
    - b. bleak
    - c. disastrous

3. What does the word *raged* mean in the context of this story?
    - a. an adopted fad or fashion
    - b. spoken very angrily
    - c. blew violently

4. Abbie becomes fearful when she sees that a nor'easter is approaching. What is a nor'easter?
    - a. a strong storm
    - b. an earthquake
    - c. a very cold temperature

5. Abbie saw a ship's light from the tower window. Which word best describes the movement of the light?
    - a. raged
    - b. flickered
    - c. swirled

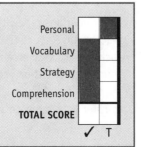

Add the numbers that you just checked to get your Personal Checklist score. Fill in your score here. Then turn to page 211 and transfer your score onto Graph 1.

Personal
Vocabulary
Strategy
Comprehension
TOTAL SCORE
✓ T

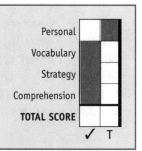

Check your answers with your teacher. Give yourself 1 point for each correct answer, and fill in your Vocabulary score here. Then turn to page 211 and transfer your score onto Graph 1.

Personal
Vocabulary
Strategy
Comprehension
TOTAL SCORE
✓ T

Strategy Check

Review the story map that you completed in the Strategy Follow-up. Also review the selection if necessary. Then answer these questions:

1. What does Abbie do just before she takes her mother and sister to the tower?
   a. She finds Jane's ball.
   b. She eases her mother's pain.
   c. She rescues Jane's hens.

2. What is another word for a story's turning point?
   a. climax
   b. conflict
   c. resolution

3. What happens after Abbie opens the tower door?
   a. She writes in her logbook.
   b. She runs to the chicken coop.
   c. She sees her father.

4. What term describes the solution to a story's problem?
   a. resolution
   b. conflict
   c. setting

5. How is Abbie's conflict in the story resolved?
   a. Abbie's father comes home and tells her that he's proud of her.
   b. Abbie's father leaves her in charge of the lighthouse.
   c. Abbie's father asks about her mother and Jane.

Comprehension Check

Review the story if necessary. Then answer these questions:

1. Why does Abbie have to take care of the household chores and her sister while her father is away?
   a. Her mother doesn't want to do anything.
   b. Her mother is sick and cannot get out of bed most days.
   c. Her mother died after Jane was born.

2. Why does Abbie want to move her mother and sister into the northern tower when the storm gets worse?
   a. She knows that her father will head for the tower.
   b. She thinks it would be easier to watch Jane in the tower.
   c. She knows that it would be unsafe to stay in their house.

3. What do Abbie, Jane, and their mother eat when they have to ration their food?
   a. roast hen
   b. cornmeal and eggs
   c. vegetables

4. When Abbie is angry, what does she see that reflects her mood?
   a. dark clouds
   b. a ship's light
   c. her father

5. How does Abbie probably feel when she snuggles in her father's arms?
   a. mad
   b. relieved
   c. frightened

Check your answers with your teacher. Give yourself 1 point for each correct answer, and fill in your Strategy score here. Then turn to page 211 and transfer your score onto Graph 1.

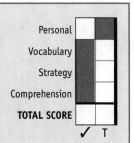

Check your answers with your teacher. Give yourself 1 point for each correct answer, and fill in your Comprehension score here. Then turn to page 211 and transfer your score onto Graph 1.

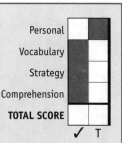

Extending

Choose one or more of these activities:

WRITE A LOGBOOK ENTRY
Imagine that you are Abbie. Complete the logbook entry that you started after the storm had passed. Describe the weather, your responsibilities, and your thoughts and feelings on your father's return.

PERFORM A SCENE
With a small group of classmates, choose a scene to perform from "The Lighthouse Keeper's Daughter." Assign roles, rehearse your parts, and perform the scene in front of your class.

LEARN ABOUT LIGHTHOUSES
Use the resources listed on this page to learn more about lighthouses. If possible, visit a lighthouse on-line and learn about it by studying the photos and reading the text. After you have visited the site, offer to take a classmate on a guided tour.

Resources

Books
Fleming, Candace. *Women of the Lights.* Whitman, 1995.

Guiberson, Brenda Z. *Lighthouses: Watchers at Sea.* Redfeather Books. Holt, 1995.

Web Sites
http://www.lighthousegetaway.com
This Web site provides information on lighthouses in the United States and Ireland.

http://www.pbs.org/legendarylighthouses
This Web site explores the history of American lighthouses. It features photographs and stories related to specific lighthouses.

Magazine
Lighthouse Digest
This monthly magazine is devoted to America's historic lighthouses. Every issue contains true stories about lighthouses and their keepers.

aground

beacon

landmark

lens

navigate

prism

shipwrecked

vessel

Lights That Guide Ships Home

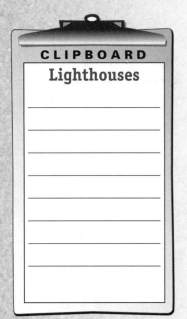

CLIPBOARD

Lighthouses

CLIPBOARD

Ships

Building Background

In "The Lighthouse Keeper's Daughter," you read about the Burgess family, who took care of a lighthouse in Maine. The story took place in the mid-1850s. Today, most modern lighthouses don't have keepers. Can you guess why? Think about what you know about lighthouses—both old and new. Then use the Venn diagram below to compare lighthouses in the past with those used today. Add more information to the diagram as you read "Lights That Guide Ships Home."

Lighthouses in the Past
• Keepers lived in or near the lighthouse.
• Lamps were lighted by oil lamps.
• Lamps were tended by keepers.

Similarities
• Lights must not go out.
• _____
  _____
  _____

Modern Lighthouses
• People don't need to live in the lighthouse.
• _____
  _____
  _____
• _____
  _____
  _____

Vocabulary Builder

1. The words in the margin are from the article you are about to read. Before you begin reading the article, decide which of the vocabulary words are related to lighthouses and which are related to ships. List each word on the appropriate clipboard.

2. As you read the article, look for other words related to lighthouses and ships. Add them to the clipboards.

3. Save your work. You will use it again in the Vocabulary Check.

Strategy Builder

Identifying Main Ideas and Supporting Details

- You may recall from Lesson 3 that an **informational article** gives facts and details about a particular **topic**. You also may recall that the topic of an article is usually stated in its title.

- Most informational articles are organized into **main ideas** and **supporting details**. These ideas and details help explain or support the topic. Read the following from an informational article on the *Titanic*. The main ideas are underlined once. The supporting details are underlined twice.

The "Unsinkable" *Titanic*

The *Titanic* was billed as the greatest ship afloat. It was the largest ship ever built, and some believed it to be the fastest. The ship also carried the very latest in wireless equipment.

   Unfortunately, people had so much confidence in the *Titanic* that they became careless. The ship's captain held the *Titanic* to a very fast speed, even though he had been warned of icebergs in the area. After the ship struck an iceberg, many people refused to believe the *Titanic* was in trouble. Even when the order was given to abandon the ship, many passengers didn't board the lifeboats.

- If you wanted to highlight the topic, main idea, and supporting details in the example above, you could put them on a graphic organizer. Here is how they would look on a **concept map**, or web:

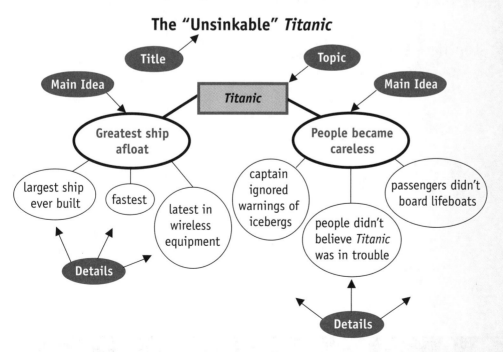

Lights That Guide Ships Home

By Lisbeth P. Sanders

As you read the first part of this informational article, you can apply some of the strategies that you just learned. Notice the underlined phrases. They contain details that support the main idea "How lighthouses bring ships safely home."

Lighthouses around the world help bring ships safely home. In darkness and in fog <u>they warn of dangerous rocks and reefs</u>. <u>They are also **landmarks**</u> by which ships find their way along the coast.

Today most lighthouses are lighted by electricity. In the majority of lighthouses, the lights run automatically. This means that no one need be there all the time.

The lantern at the top of a lighthouse is its most important part. The light inside is enclosed in a giant glass **lens**. The lens turns around the light. **Prisms** on the lens help bend the light's rays into a single blazing beam. This forms <u>a **beacon** that helps sailors **navigate**</u>.

By day, sailors know a lighthouse by its size, shape, and color. By night, they know a lighthouse by its beacon and the color or pattern of the light. Although the light is usually white, sometimes it is colored.

Some beacons show a fixed steady light. Others flash their light in a special pattern as the lens revolves around the lamp. A flashing pattern has periods of dark and light. In some patterns, the periods of dark are longer. In others, the periods of light are longer.

 Stop here for the Strategy Break.

Strategy Break

If you stopped to arrange the main idea and supporting details in the preceding paragraphs on a concept map, they might look like this:

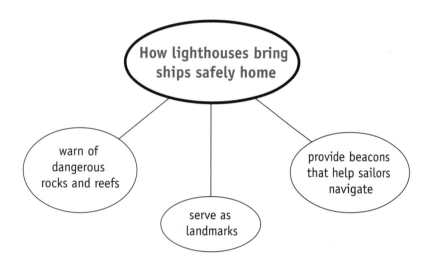

As you continue reading, keep paying attention to the article's main ideas and supporting details. When you finish reading, you will use some of those ideas and details to create a concept map of your own.

 Go on reading.

Kerosene was used as fuel for years in lighthouse lamps. It made a bright light, although it was a dirty fuel. The smoky lamps had to be cleaned each day and the wicks had to be trimmed. So the people who took care of the lights came to be known as wickies.

Many stories are told about the brave wickies. Besides tending their lamps, they rescued people who were **shipwrecked** in dangerous seas. The families of wickies lived in the lighthouses, too, and were often lonely.

There are many lighthouses in use today. One lighthouse built on a dangerous reef is the Eddystone Light in the English Channel. Its lantern rises 135 feet (41 meters) above the water.

There have been four Eddystone Lights. The first was built in 1694. It was a fancy tower of wood and stone. The man who built it was proud of his tower, but he didn't know how to build a lighthouse that would stand in rough seas. One night in a terrible storm the tower was washed away with its builder inside. Sturdier lighthouses were built later.

The fourth lighthouse, finished in 1882, was built to withstand storms. It still stands today—nine stories tall. On top is a huge lantern lighted by electricity.

Another lighthouse is Portland Head Light. It was built in 1787. It stands in Portland Harbor in Maine, guiding ships away from danger.

One wintry night in 1864 there was a heavy fog. A ship was bringing people from Ireland to live in America. The fog kept the captain from seeing the Portland Head Light.

The ship crashed into a huge rock in the sea. The passengers got into lifeboats. They were lowered over the side of the ship. Most of them were saved from what nearly was a terrible disaster.

One person saved that night was a boy named John F. Fitzgerald. He grew up to become mayor of Boston. His grandson, John Fitzgerald Kennedy, was the thirty-fifth president of the United States.

Lighthouses are needed along the Pacific coast too. One night in 1853, in a thick fog, a clipper ship named *Carrier Pigeon* went **aground** near Whale Point, California. The crew got to shore safely. But the ship could not be saved. There was no lighthouse to help the sailors find their way.

The people did not forget the wreck of the lovely ship. They gave Whale Point a new name. They called it Pigeon Point. Other wrecks happened. Eighteen years after the *Carrier Pigeon* was lost, a lighthouse was finally built. It was inspired by the need to save other ships.

Pigeon Point Lighthouse is still a landmark for ships entering San Francisco Bay. It is a helpful guide that ships' captains rely on.

In fog, lighthouses signal to ships at sea with lights, horns, or whistles. They send signals over electronic equipment, which can be received by any **vessel** with the proper radio apparatus. Lighthouses also make use of other aids to ships. Many have radio beacons that send out Morse code characteristics at certain times and on a particular frequency.

There are about 400 lighthouses in the United States. They protect shipping on the coasts, on the Great Lakes, and on some rivers too. The United States Coast Guard is in charge of maintaining all aids to navigation, which include lighthouses. ●

Strategy Follow-up

Now create a concept map for the paragraphs that describe the shipwreck off Portland Head Light in 1864. (They begin on page 52, paragraph 3.) The main idea has been filled in for you.

Shipwreck off Portland Head Light: 1864

✓Personal Checklist

Read each question and put a check (✓) in the correct box.

1. Before you read the article, how many vocabulary words were you able to place on the appropriate clipboards?
   - ☐ 3 (6–8 words)
   - ☐ 2 (3–5 words)
   - ☐ 1 (0–2 words)

2. In Building Background, you compared lighthouses in the past with modern lighthouses. How well were you able to find details that supported your ideas?
   - ☐ 3 (extremely well)
   - ☐ 2 (fairly well)
   - ☐ 1 (not well)

3. How well do you understand the information in this article?
   - ☐ 3 (extremely well)
   - ☐ 2 (fairly well)
   - ☐ 1 (not well)

4. How well were you able to complete the concept map in the Strategy Follow-up?
   - ☐ 3 (extremely well)
   - ☐ 2 (fairly well)
   - ☐ 1 (not well)

5. How well do you understand the importance of lighthouses?
   - ☐ 3 (extremely well)
   - ☐ 2 (fairly well)
   - ☐ 1 (not well)

Vocabulary Check

Look back at the work you did in the Vocabulary Builder. Then answer each question by circling the correct letter.

1. Which word belongs on a list of words related to lighthouses?
   a. landmark
   b. aground
   c. shipwrecked

2. Lighthouses help sailors navigate. What does *navigate* mean?
   a. rescue those lost at sea
   b. stay awake
   c. find their way through the water

3. Which of the following does *not* have to do with the lantern in a lighthouse?
   a. vessel
   b. prism
   c. lens

4. The beacon from a lighthouse helps sailors navigate. Which context clue might have helped you figure out what *beacon* means?
   a. "its most important part"
   b. "a giant glass lens"
   c. "a single blazing beam"

5. What happens when a ship runs aground?
   a. It runs out of fuel.
   b. It becomes stuck on or near shore.
   c. It runs over the ground.

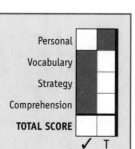

Add the numbers that you just checked to get your Personal Checklist score. Fill in your score here. Then turn to page 211 and transfer your score onto Graph 1.

	Personal	
	Vocabulary	
	Strategy	
	Comprehension	
	TOTAL SCORE	
	✓	T

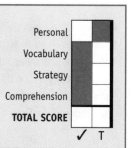

Check your answers with your teacher. Give yourself 1 point for each correct answer, and fill in your Vocabulary score here. Then turn to page 211 and transfer your score onto Graph 1.

	Personal	
	Vocabulary	
	Strategy	
	Comprehension	
	TOTAL SCORE	
	✓	T

Strategy Check

Review the concept map that you completed in the Strategy Follow-up. Also review the selection if necessary. Then answer these questions:

1. Which of the following details could you have included on your concept map?
   a. first was built in 1694
   b. ship bringing people from Ireland
   c. no lighthouse to help the sailors

2. Who was one of the passengers on the ship that crashed off Portland Head Light?
   a. President John F. Kennedy's grandfather
   b. President John F. Kennedy
   c. the man who built the lighthouse

3. What happened to the people on board the ship that crashed off Portland Head Light?
   a. They were all killed.
   b. They got into lifeboats and were saved.
   c. The crew got to shore safely, but the passengers were killed.

4. Which of the following details could appear on a concept map in which the main idea is "the shipwreck of the *Carrier Pigeon*"?
   a. Whale Point was renamed Pigeon Point in honor of the ship.
   b. The wreck occurred in 1787.
   c. Fog kept the ship's captain from seeing the lighthouse.

5. Which detail does *not* support the main idea "the history of the Eddystone Light"?
   a. The first tower was washed away in a terrible storm.
   b. The fourth lighthouse still stands today.
   c. The lighthouse serves as a landmark for ships entering San Francisco Bay.

Comprehension Check

Review the article if necessary. Then answer these questions:

1. Why don't lighthouse keepers live in lighthouses anymore?
   a. Modern lighthouses are too small.
   b. Modern lighthouses are too dangerous.
   c. Modern lighthouses run automatically and use electricity.

2. What is the most important part of a lighthouse?
   a. the lantern at the top of a lighthouse
   b. the color of the lighthouse
   c. the shape of the lighthouse

3. What was one of the drawbacks of using kerosene to fuel lighthouse lamps?
   a. It made a bright light.
   b. It was a dirty fuel.
   c. It was used for years.

4. How do modern lighthouses send signals to ships at sea when fog is present?
   a. using kerosene lights
   b. using electric lights
   c. using electronic equipment

5. Who is in charge of maintaining all of the lighthouses in the United States?
   a. the United States Navy
   b. the United States Coast Guard
   c. individual lighthouse keepers

Check your answers with your teacher. Give yourself 1 point for each correct answer, and fill in your Strategy score here. Then turn to page 211 and transfer your score onto Graph 1.

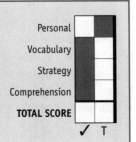

Personal
Vocabulary
Strategy
Comprehension
TOTAL SCORE
✓ T

Check your answers with your teacher. Give yourself 1 point for each correct answer, and fill in your Comprehension score here. Then turn to page 211 and transfer your score onto Graph 1.

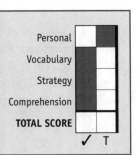

Personal
Vocabulary
Strategy
Comprehension
TOTAL SCORE
✓ T

Extending

Choose one or both of these activities:

DRAW A LIGHTHOUSE

Draw a picture of one of the lighthouses named in the article, or another one you're interested in. Visit the library or use the resources listed on this page. Then make a poster-sized drawing of the lighthouse and label its most important parts.

WRITE AN ARTICLE ABOUT A SHIPWRECK

Find out more about one of the shipwrecks mentioned in the article, or research another shipwreck. Then write a brief newspaper article in which you tell when and where the wreck took place, why it happened, and how many people were hurt.

Resources

Books

Allen, William. *Accounts of Shipwrecks and Other Disasters.* Notable American Authors. Reprint Services, 1981.

De Wire, Elinore. *The Lighthouse Activity Book.* Sentinel Publications, 1995.

Platt, Richard. *Shipwreck.* Eyewitness. DK Publishing, 2000.

Web Sites

http://www.lsgb.co.uk/
This is the Web site of the Lighthouse Society of Great Britain. Click on "An Eddystone Visit" for information about the Eddystone Light.

http://www.portlandheadlight.com/
Learn about the Portland Head Light on this Web site.

http://www.rudyalicelighthouse.net/CalLts/PigeonPt/PigeonPt.htm
This Web site contains information about the Pigeon Point Lighthouse.

Video/DVD

The Lighthouses of New England. Bfs Entertainment, 1998.

Learning New Words

VOCABULARY

From Lesson 2
- bent my ear
- call it even
- caught me off balance
- lend a hand
- packed it in
- pulled one over on
- wearing thin

Idioms

An idiom is an expression that can't be understood by the meanings of the individual words, but you can figure out the meaning from the context of the sentence. For example, when Ben first meets Charlie in "Charlie Johnson," Ben thinks, "I had been ready for a lecture, even for some yelling and screaming, but this *caught me off balance.*" In this context, the meaning of the idiom *caught me off balance* is "surprised me."

Write the idiom that means the same as the words in boldface below.

1. My father wanted me to **help**. _____

2. The circus **stopped performing and left**. _____

3. Greg **talked to me endlessly** about his homework. _____

4. She really **fooled** her little brother. _____

5. My friend's same excuses every time were **getting old**. _____

Compound Words

A compound word is made of two words put together. In "Lights That Guide Ships Home," the author talks about how important lighthouses are in preventing a shipwreck. *Shipwreck* is made from the words *ship* and *wreck* and means "the event of wrecking a ship."

Fill in each blank with a compound word by combining a word from Row 1 with a word from Row 2.

Row 1: shoe   book   air   dish   snow

Row 2: suit   washer   plane   shelf   lace

1. machine to clean plates = _____

2. baby's winter clothing = _____

3. a place to put books = _____

4. a craft that travels in the sky = _____

5. used to tie your sneakers = _____

Antonyms

An antonym is a word that means the opposite of another word. In "How Buildings Take Shape," the author uses the words *horizontal* and *vertical* to describe opposite types of lines that architects use in drawing buildings. Horizontal lines run across the page, while vertical lines run from the top of the page to the bottom.

Draw a line from each word in Column 1 to its antonym in Column 2.

Column 1	Column 2
long	simple
quiet	cheap
interesting	loud
expensive	short
complicated	boring

VOCABULARY

From Lesson 1
- breakaway
- defenseman

From Lesson 5
- landmark
- shipwrecked

From Lesson 3
- horizontal/ vertical

LESSON 6 Dancing the Cotton-Eyed Joe

Building Background

The story you are about to read is called "Dancing the Cotton-Eyed Joe." Mark, the main character in the story, learns how to dance the Cotton-Eyed Joe from someone unusual. Think about a time you learned how to do something from someone you didn't think could teach you. For instance, maybe a grandparent taught you a new song, or a younger brother or sister showed you how to find a site on the Web. On a separate sheet of paper, answer these questions:

- What did you learn?

- Who taught you how to do it?

- What did the experience teach you?

complicated

entrance

ghost town

pestered

rude

specialty

Vocabulary Builder

1. Like most words, the vocabulary words in the margin have antonyms and synonyms. **Antonyms** are words with opposite meanings. **Synonyms** are words with similar meanings. Knowing a word's antonym or synonym can help you learn and remember the word.

2. Each boldfaced vocabulary word on page 61 is followed by two other words or phrases. One of the two words or phrases is an antonym of the boldfaced word.

3. Before you begin reading the selection, underline the antonyms of the bold-faced words. Use a dictionary if necessary.

4. Save your work. You will use it again in the Vocabulary Check.

complicated	simple	complex
entrance	opening	exit
ghost town	busy city	deserted area
pestered	left alone	annoyed
rude	impolite	courteous
specialty	inability	talent

Strategy Builder

Drawing Conclusions While Reading a Story

- A **conclusion** is a decision that you reach after thinking about certain facts or information. When you read a story, you often **draw conclusions** based on information that the author gives you about the characters, setting, and events.

- Since fiction is often based on real life, the **setting** and **characters** play an important role. You can use information about the setting and characters to draw conclusions about the character's lives, their feelings, and their experiences.

- Read the following paragraph from "Dancing the Cotton-Eyed Joe." See if you can draw any conclusions about the narrator's life.

> At the south end of the room was a little stage for the band. Mrs. Madrid plays the upright piano, and Mr. Madrid plays fiddle. My dad plays guitar, and my mom sits behind her little drum set and beats out the rhythm. Dad's guitar case was lying open beside Mom's feet. I remember when my youngest sister, Julie, was a baby, and she slept in the guitar case. Mom says I slept there, too, when I was a baby.

- After reading the paragraph, what conclusions can you draw about the narrator and his family? Here are some conclusions that one reader drew:

First, I can conclude that the narrator's parents love music, since they both play in a band. I also can conclude that the narrator and his sister have grown up with music in their lives. When they were babies, they both slept in their father's guitar case while their parents played. Finally, I can conclude that the family probably lives in a small town. The band is small, the other two members of the band are a married couple, and babies are allowed on stage.

Dancing the Cotton-Eyed Joe

By Joann Mazzio

As you read the first part of this story, see what conclusions you can draw about the characters and the setting. Pay attention to the information that the author gives you to help you draw your conclusions.

I've been coming to country-western dances at Lake Valley since I was a baby. As soon as I was big enough to walk, I was trying to dance. I'm thirteen now and I've learned the two-step, the waltz, and the polka. I've even learned to dance the schottische.

But until one night in January, I didn't know how to dance the Cotton-Eyed Joe. On the night I learned that dance, I learned something else, too.

On that winter night, the air in Lake Valley was like black velvet. That's because Lake Valley is a **ghost town**. No one lives there. But then, at 8:30 sharp, my dad turned on the lights in the old brick schoolhouse. It was like magic. Light streamed from the windows, and you could see people gathered outside the building. All kinds of folks come to the Saturday night dances—old people, young couples, and families with babies. In the shadows around the building were cars, RVs, and pickups splattered with mud from ranch roads.

Mrs. Jessup and Mrs. Taylor sat at the door collecting admission. I was carrying the pot of baked beans Mom had given me to take inside the schoolhouse.

I put the beans down at the **entrance** and stuck out my hand to be stamped. I don't have to pay admission because my mom and dad are in the band. But ever since I was a little kid, Mrs. Jessup or Mrs. Taylor has been stamping the back of my hand so that it says "Lake Valley Dance." It's like a ticket saying you've paid.

Mrs. Taylor said, "Well, Mark, have you learned to dance the Cotton-Eyed Joe yet?"

"No, Mrs. Taylor," I said. "I'm waiting for you to teach me."

"Oh, if it weren't for this arthritis in my knees, I'd have you dancing it in no time."

"That's right, Mark," Mrs. Jessup said. "That was Eula's **specialty**. If I didn't have this dad-blamed walker, I'd teach you myself."

"Have a good time tonight, honey," said Mrs. Taylor.

At the north end of the long room stood a table for the food people had brought. I dodged through the crowd to put our baked beans there.

Parents were setting up playpens and putting sleepy babies in them. The coat hooks were filled, so people piled their wraps on the benches around the room.

At the south end of the room was a little stage for the band. Mrs. Madrid plays the upright piano, and Mr. Madrid plays fiddle. My dad plays guitar, and my mom sits behind her little drum set and beats out the rhythm. Dad's guitar case was lying open beside Mom's feet. I remember when my youngest sister, Julie, was a baby, and she slept in the guitar case. Mom says I slept there, too, when I was a baby.

Though the band had started to play, Julie was up onstage saying something to Mom. Mom nodded her head in my direction, and Julie came running over. She begged me to dance with her. I was teaching her to do the dances I knew. Country-western dancing is not like square-dancing. There's no caller to tell you what to do; you have to know the steps yourself.

First Julie and I danced a polka. After that was over, the band played Ten Pretty Girls. Now, this dance is like the Cotton-Eyed Joe. It's got a lot of **complicated** moves in it. Julie **pestered** me to teach her, but I said, "You'll have to get someone else, Julie. I don't know it."

"Dad should be the one to teach me," Julie said. She was right. Usually mothers teach their sons, and fathers teach the daughters.

Just then Julie saw one of her friends and ran over to join her. I sat down on a bench. Across the room from me, I saw a stranger—a girl about my age sitting alone.

 Stop here for the Strategy Break.

Strategy Break

What conclusions can you draw about this story so far? Using information from the story and what you learned in the Strategy Builder, try to answer the following questions. The hints below each question will help you draw your conclusions.

1. What can you conclude about where Mark and his family live?
   Hint: Think about the details he uses to describe the setting and the people who come to the dances. _____

   _____

2. Why do so many people come to the dances?
   Hint: Think about how Mark describes the dances, and also try to imagine what life must be like where he lives. _____

   _____

3. What kind of person is Mark?
   Hint: Think about how he talks to Mrs. Taylor and Mrs. Jessup, and how he treats his sister.

   _____

   _____

As you continue reading, keep paying attention to the information that the author gives you about the characters and setting. At the end of the story, you will be asked to draw more conclusions.

 Go on reading to see what happens.

Most everyone at the dance wore Western shirts and jeans and cowboy boots. But this girl had on a long-sleeved dress that covered her knees. Her hair hung straight and blond. She looked like Alice in Wonderland.

I worked my way around the end of the room, staying out of the way of the dancing couples.

When I stood in front of her, she didn't look up at me until I spoke. "Hello," I said. "This is your first time here, isn't it?"

She looked at me with wide-open misty blue eyes. "Yes," she said. "I'm visiting my aunt and uncle in Las Cruces. They brought me tonight because I love country-western dancing. My name's Alice."

That's easy to remember, I thought. "My name's Mark," I said. "They're starting to play a polka now. Would you like to dance?"

I held out my hand to her and waited until she put her hand up. I took hold of it and held it until she stood. Her blue eyes did not look into mine, but stared past my right ear. Then she did a strange thing. With her free hand, she felt my shoulder, then my neck, then touched the top of my head.

"So I know how tall you are," she said.

I dropped her hand as if it were a hot potato. "You're blind," I said. Then I knew how **rude** that was. But I'd never been around blind people. I didn't know how you're supposed to talk to them or treat them.

"I'm sorry," I said. "I didn't know. You probably don't want to dance. You might get hurt in this crowd."

"Don't be silly," she said. "I can dance very well. I just need a partner to guide me. Don't you want to?" Her voice sounded as if she were daring me.

"Sure." I put my arm around her waist very lightly and just barely touched her hand.

"For goodness sakes, I'm not going to break. Take a good hold of me. I'm just like any other girl you might dance with," she said. "Blindness is a bother when I want to read or when I'm buying a dress, but it's no bother here."

I took her at her word. I figured she knew a lot more about being blind than I did. I swung her out into the middle of the room and found myself dancing better than I ever had before. The polka steps came out of my legs and feet as easy as the rhythm from my mom's drums.

"That was great," I said and held her hand to show her that I wanted her to be my partner for the next dance.

When the music started again, it was the Cotton-Eyed Joe. I was disappointed because now I had to let her go. Someone else would want to dance with her because she was so good. I led her to the bench where she had been sitting.

"Don't you want to dance this one?" Alice asked.

"I don't know how."

"I'll teach you." She pulled my arms until they were in the right place and our hands were held just so. "Now, watch my feet and listen." We joined the other couples circling the dance floor.

"Now put your left hand around my waist and your right out front," she whispered. She was a good teacher. I don't believe I ever learned anything so fast in my life.

When other boys saw how good she was, they started asking her to dance. Then the band played Ten Pretty Girls, and I got her to teach me that dance, too.

At midnight the band stopped playing, and we lined up at the table to fill our plates with food. I helped Alice get what she wanted on her plate.

While we ate, Alice told silly elephant jokes. I can't remember them, but she must have known a hundred. We laughed and had fun.

The next day I thought about what I had learned. Making a new friend is sort of like magic. Like Lake Valley on a Saturday night. You're in a dark place. Then the lights go on. And a ghost town comes alive with music and dancing. ●

Strategy Follow-up

Use the information in the story to help you answer these questions:

1. Mark walks over to Alice and asks her to dance. From the details he gives, what can you conclude about his reasons for doing so?

   _____

   _____

2. Alice doesn't get angry when Mark drops her hand and says, "You're blind." What does this help you conclude about Alice's experiences with people?

   _____

   _____

3. Mark dances with Alice even though he says he doesn't know how to treat blind people. What does this help you conclude about Mark?

   _____

   _____

4. Alice doesn't let her blindness stop her from having fun. What does this help you conclude about her personality?

   _____

   _____

✓Personal Checklist

Read each question and put a check (✓) in the correct box.

1. How well do you understand what the country-western dances at Lake Valley were like?
   - ☐ 3 (extremely well)
   - ☐ 2 (fairly well)
   - ☐ 1 (not well)

2. How many antonyms did you correctly underline in the Vocabulary Builder?
   - ☐ 3 (5–6 words)
   - ☐ 2 (3–4 words)
   - ☐ 1 (0–2 words)

3. How well were you able to draw conclusions about the characters and setting in the story?
   - ☐ 3 (extremely well)
   - ☐ 2 (fairly well)
   - ☐ 1 (not well)

4. How well do you understand why Alice wanted to dance?
   - ☐ 3 (extremely well)
   - ☐ 2 (fairly well)
   - ☐ 1 (not well)

5. How well do you understand what else Mark learned on the night he learned the Cotton-Eyed Joe?
   - ☐ 3 (extremely well)
   - ☐ 2 (fairly well)
   - ☐ 1 (not well)

Vocabulary Check

Look back at the work you did in the Vocabulary Builder. Then answer each question by circling the correct letter.

1. Which word is a synonym of *annoyed*?
   a. complicated
   b. pestered
   c. enjoyed

2. Which word is an antonym of *exit*?
   a. ghost town
   b. specialty
   c. entrance

3. Julie begs Mark to teach her how to dance Ten Pretty Girls. Which word best describes her behavior?
   a. pestered
   b. rude
   c. specialty

4. Mark describes Lake Valley as a ghost town. What is an antonym of *ghost town*?
   a. deserted area
   b. haunted area
   c. busy city

5. Mrs. Taylor's specialty was dancing the Cotton-Eyed Joe. What is an antonym of *specialty*?
   a. talent
   b. inability
   c. favorite

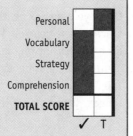

Add the numbers that you just checked to get your Personal Checklist score. Fill in your score here. Then turn to page 211 and transfer your score onto Graph 1.

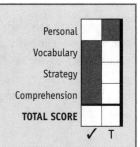

Check your answers with your teacher. Give yourself 1 point for each correct answer, and fill in your Vocabulary score here. Then turn to page 211 and transfer your score onto Graph 1.

Strategy Check

Review the conclusions you drew in the Strategy Break and Strategy Follow-up. Also review the selection if necessary. Then answer these questions:

1. Which statement best describes Mark's first response to Alice?

   a. He felt nothing special toward her.

   b. He wanted to know her.

   c. He felt no attraction to her at all.

2. Mark drops Alice's hand when he finds out that she is blind. What can you conclude from his behavior?

   a. He hadn't realized that she was blind.

   b. He doesn't like blind people.

   c. He's afraid of blind people.

3. Why does Mark hold Alice very gently when they first begin to dance?

   a. He doesn't want to touch her.

   b. He's afraid that she will break.

   c. He doesn't know how to treat her.

4. When the Cotton-Eyed Joe plays, Mark leads Alice back to her seat, but she wants to keep dancing. What can you conclude from this?

   a. Alice likes Mark and wants to keep dancing with him.

   b. Mark doesn't want to dance with Alice anymore.

   c. Alice is afraid to be by herself.

5. On the night of the dance, Mark learned to dance the Cotton-Eyed Joe. What else did he learn?

   a. that blind people are good dancers

   b. that making a new friend is magical

   c. that he's a good dancer

Comprehension Check

Review the story if necessary. Then answer these questions:

1. What's unusual about Lake Valley?

   a. It's the country-western dance capital of the world.

   b. No one lives there.

   c. It's haunted.

2. Why has Mark come to the dances since he was a baby?

   a. His parents play in the band, and he loves to dance.

   b. Mark plays in the band.

   c. He has to help bring the food.

3. Why does Mark think that Alice looks like Alice in Wonderland?

   a. because she has misty blue eyes

   b. because she's wearing a Western shirt, jeans, and cowboy boots

   c. because she's wearing a long-sleeved dress and has straight, blond hair

4. What does Mark discover when he dances with Alice?

   a. that she dances very well

   b. that she's blind

   c. that she doesn't know how to dance the Cotton-Eyed Joe

5. Why was that January dance so special to Mark?

   a. He learned some new jokes.

   b. He finally learned the Cotton-Eyed Joe, and he made a friend.

   c. He made the other boys jealous.

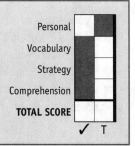

Check your answers with your teacher. Give yourself 1 point for each correct answer, and fill in your Strategy score here. Then turn to page 211 and transfer your score onto Graph 1.

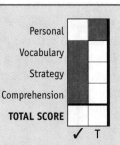

Check your answers with your teacher. Give yourself 1 point for each correct answer, and fill in your Comprehension score here. Then turn to page 211 and transfer your score onto Graph 1.

Extending

Choose one or both of these activities:

LEARN A COUNTRY-WESTERN DANCE

Choose a dance from the story. Then, with a partner, explore the resources listed on this page and find out how to perform the dance. After you and your partner have mastered the steps, teach your classmates the dance. If you have a video camera, you can also make a "how-to" video.

LISTEN TO COUNTRY MUSIC

Listen to one of the recordings listed on this page, or search the Web for other suggestions. Play some of the songs that you find for your classmates. If you can read music or play an instrument, learn a country-western dance song and play it for your class.

Resources

Web Sites

http://www.ibiblio.org/schools/rls/dances/
This Web site has a large library of country western dances. Click on "List of 10,000+ Dance Files." This list of dance instructions includes instructions for dancing the Cotton-Eyed Joe.

Audio Recordings

Cotton-Eyed Joe! Texas Dance Favorites! Instrumentals. Landmark, 1999.

Heroes of Country Music, Vol. 1: Legends of Western Swing. Rhino Records, 1996.

South Texas Polka Party: 16 Polka Instrumentals. Arhoolie, 1997.

Videos/DVDs

Christy Lane's Surviving the Country Dance Floor: A Guide to Partner Dancing. Christy Lane. Brentwood Home Video, 1993.

Country Western Dancing. Dance Lessons for Beginners. Fred Astaire Dance Studios. Best Film & Video, 1990.

Lucky to Be Alive

Building Background

In the selection you are about to read, the author tells about her experiences during a terrible lightning storm. What do you know about lightning? You've probably seen lightning flash during a storm. You may even know what you're supposed to do if you're outside during a lightning storm—where you should go and where you shouldn't go. Get together with a partner and discuss what you know about lightning. Also, share any personal experiences or memories of lightning storms you might have witnessed.

current

film

limbs

shaken

skirt

strained

Vocabulary Builder

1. Words that have more than one meaning are called **multiple-meaning words**. For example, the word *branch* can mean "a tree limb" or "a department within a business" or "an offshoot of a river." To figure out which meaning of a word an author is using, you have to use context.

2. The vocabulary words in the margin are all multiple-meaning words. The words are listed below, followed by some of their different meanings. As you read the selection, use context to figure out which meaning is the one the author is using. Circle the letter of the correct meaning.

3. Save your work. You will use it again in the Vocabulary Check.

current	a. fashionable	b. flow of a river	c. electricity
film	a. movie	b. thin coating	c. thin skin
limbs	a. arms	b. legs	c. branches of a tree
shaken	a. violently moved	b. upset	c. clasped hands in greeting
skirt	a. to go around	b. part of a dress	c. avoided or ignored
strained	a. tried hard	b. injured	c. filtered

Strategy Builder

Identifying Causes and Effects

- Many pieces of writing contain cause-and-effect relationships. A **cause** tells *why* something happened. An **effect** tells *what* happened.

- To find a cause-and-effect relationship while you read, ask yourself, "What happened?" and "Why did it happen?" This will help you understand what has happened in the selection so far. It also will help you predict what might happen next.

- As you read the following paragraph, think about what happens, and why.

> As Erin was walking home from school, rain suddenly began to fall very hard. She didn't have an umbrella, so her clothes became soaked. Soon the rain made her clothes so heavy that she had to walk very slowly. As a result, Erin was late getting home. She didn't have time to change for her swimming lesson. Her mother spread a blanket on the car seat and drove Erin to the pool. When Erin walked in, everyone asked her if she swam there.

- If you wanted to track the causes and effects in this paragraph, you could put them on a **cause-and-effect chain**. It might look like this:

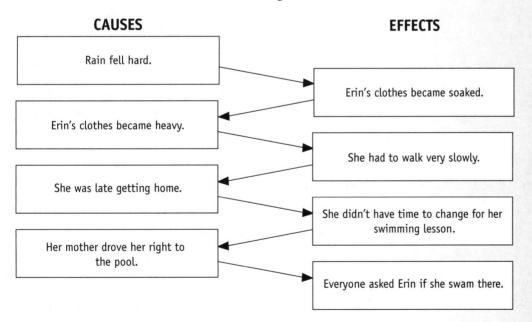

CAUSES

Rain fell hard.

Erin's clothes became heavy.

She was late getting home.

Her mother drove her right to the pool.

EFFECTS

Erin's clothes became soaked.

She had to walk very slowly.

She didn't have time to change for her swimming lesson.

Everyone asked Erin if she swam there.

Lucky to Be Alive

By Carol Ann Moorhead

As you read the first part of this personal account, you can apply the strategies that you just learned. To find the causes and effects, keep asking yourself, "What happened?" and "Why did it happen?"

Despite Chicken Little's insistence that "the sky is falling, the sky is falling," I never believed him. When I was a young child, the sky was as secure above my head as the ground was beneath my feet. That was before I felt the earth quake, and before I learned that Chicken Little is sometimes right.

My sky fell one summer evening in Massachusetts. It did not fall all at once, nor without warning. It heaved and cracked with the roll of thunder of an approaching storm. It shattered into pieces with cloud-to-cloud lightning as a few raindrops began to fall. My friend Bill and I hurried down a woodland path, making jokes about lightning and trying to remember tips about lightning safety. Not to worry, we assured ourselves. This isn't a bad storm. As if to prove us wrong, the winds picked up. Black clouds rolled in, releasing rains so heavy that we were soaked within seconds. Our clothes clung to our bodies, and our feet sloshed through instant puddles. We fell silent, fearful of the storm upon us.

Behind us bright bolts of lightning began probing the woodlands, lighting up the forest, and sparking our conversation. We made a plan: Exit the forest, **skirt** its edge, and re-enter on the other path. The other path, I knew from a previous hike, would quickly lead us to an abandoned car. It was the best option. The storm was gaining on us, and my own car was across an open meadow at least four football fields long.

The sky was so dark now that we could barely see. Carefully we made our way out of the forest and along its edge. Suddenly, BAM! There was an explosion of white light at my feet. I felt a sharp thrust upward, and then heard a muffled thump.

I landed on my back: Ears ringing and skin tingling, I struggled to roll onto my feet, but my legs couldn't lift me. I squatted in the darkness, trembling, and shouting, "Bill! Are you okay?! Bill!"

Bill didn't answer. I **strained** my eyes to see if I could see him lying near me. If I could only crawl to him I could help, I thought, but I could see nothing but darkness. Seconds ticked by, maybe minutes. Slowly I raised myself into a skier's crouch. I shouted again, and suddenly a wet hug answered my call.

"I couldn't answer," he said. "The muscles around my mouth wouldn't move. Come on. Let's go!"

 Stop here for the Strategy Break.

Strategy Break

If you were to create a cause-and-effect chain for this personal account so far, it might look like this:

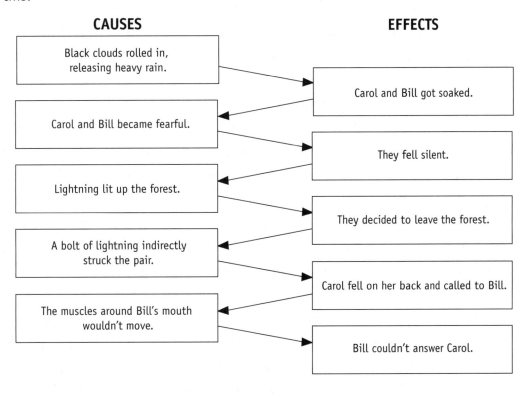

CAUSES

EFFECTS

Black clouds rolled in, releasing heavy rain.

Carol and Bill got soaked.

Carol and Bill became fearful.

They fell silent.

Lightning lit up the forest.

They decided to leave the forest.

A bolt of lightning indirectly struck the pair.

Carol fell on her back and called to Bill.

The muscles around Bill's mouth wouldn't move.

Bill couldn't answer Carol.

Go on reading to see what happens.

By now, the storm was centered above us. A second bolt hit the forest, then a third. Like shell-shocked soldiers, we fell to our knees each time. A fourth bolt. I don't recall being afraid, only angry—angry at this deranged storm that seemed determined to find us. Luckily, on the fifth bolt I saw the silhouette of a small car. "Oh, please," I thought, "let it be unlocked."

Bill lifted the handle. To our relief, it unlatched. We piled inside the abandoned car and shut the door. Finally we were safe. We pinched ourselves and poked each other to make sure we were alive. Our legs trembled and tingled for over an hour as we waited out the storm. Bill complained of a sharp pain on the ball of his foot. My feet ached all over. Once the storm seemed safely past, we walked on wobbly legs back to my car and drove home to my sister's house. By the time we arrived, we felt less **shaken**. Despite her encouragement, we decided not to go to the emergency room.

The next day Bill and I walked back to the site where we had been struck. A mangled birch tree stood beside the path. Its trunk was split wide open, and a black streak blazed its otherwise yellow insides. Several broken **limbs** hung to the ground.

Suddenly my eyes settled on four dead grassy spots along the path, only 2 meters from the tree. Our footprints! We guessed that these were the points where the electricity entered and exited our bodies.

Bill and I knew that we'd been lucky, but just how lucky, we didn't know until later that week when we visited the Boston Museum of Science. The museum had just opened a lightning demonstration and we couldn't resist going. Using large generators, scientists created electrical strikes that looked like lightning bolts, right inside the museum! Bill ducked at the first strike and I jumped. Despite knowing we were safe behind a shield of grounded wires, it was hard not to be scared.

After the demonstration, Bill and I approached one of the scientists. We told him our story, described the dead grassy spots, and showed him the burn marks on our sandaled feet. "You're lucky to be alive," he said, shaking his head. "If you hadn't been walking, you might not be here today."

The scientist explained that we had survived an indirect lightning strike. The bolt had hit the tree, traveled through the ground, entered one foot and exited the other. Had we been standing with our legs together, instead of walking, the **current** might have struck our hearts and other organs, perhaps killing us because we had been so close to the tree. He added that being soaking wet may also have helped. Much like the car's metal exterior, the thin **film** of water coating our skin may have allowed some of the current to pass around us, rather than through us.

Bill and I left the museum, once again pinching ourselves and poking each other. It was a beautiful sunny day and we were grateful to be alive. ●

Strategy Follow-up

Complete this cause-and-effect chain for the second part of the selection. Copy it onto another sheet of paper if you need more room to write. Some of the chain has been filled in for you.

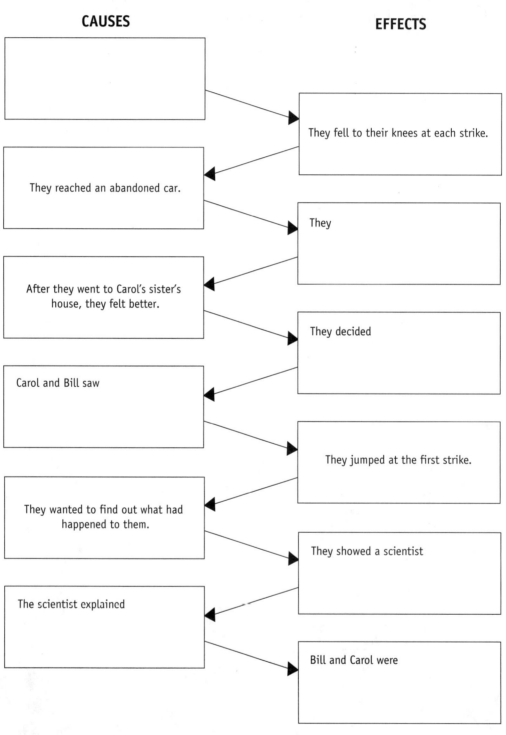

CAUSES

EFFECTS

They fell to their knees at each strike.

They reached an abandoned car.

They

After they went to Carol's sister's house, they felt better.

They decided

Carol and Bill saw

They jumped at the first strike.

They wanted to find out what had happened to them.

They showed a scientist

The scientist explained

Bill and Carol were

✓Personal Checklist

Read each question and put a check (✓) in the correct box.

1. How well did your discussion of lightning in Building Background help you understand what happened in the selection?
   - ☐ 3 (extremely well)
   - ☐ 2 (fairly well)
   - ☐ 1 (not well)

2. In the Vocabulary Builder, how well were you able to match the words with the meanings that the author used?
   - ☐ 3 (extremely well)
   - ☐ 2 (fairly well)
   - ☐ 1 (not well)

3. How well were you able to identify the causes and effects in the selection?
   - ☐ 3 (extremely well)
   - ☐ 2 (fairly well)
   - ☐ 1 (not well)

4. How well do you understand why Carol and Bill survived the lightning strike?
   - ☐ 3 (extremely well)
   - ☐ 2 (fairly well)
   - ☐ 1 (not well)

5. How well do you understand why Carol and Bill were grateful when they left the museum?
   - ☐ 3 (extremely well)
   - ☐ 2 (fairly well)
   - ☐ 1 (not well)

Vocabulary Check

Look back at the work you did in the Vocabulary Builder. Then answer each question by circling the correct letter.

1. Which vocabulary word in the selection is used to mean "to go around"?
   - a. shaken
   - b. strained
   - c. skirt

2. The lightning's current might have killed Carol and Bill if they had been standing still. Which meaning of *current* does the author use?
   - a. fashionable
   - b. flow of a river
   - c. electricity

3. *His dirty hand left a film of grease around the cup.* Which meaning of the word *film* is used in this sentence?
   - a. thin coating
   - b. thin skin
   - c. movie

4. The author says that several broken limbs hung to the ground where lightning had struck. Which meaning of *limbs* does the author use?
   - a. arms
   - b. branches of a tree
   - c. legs

5. If you said that you strained to see your friend marching in a parade, which meaning of *strained* would you be using?
   - a. injured
   - b. filtered
   - c. tried hard

Add the numbers that you just checked to get your Personal Checklist score. Fill in your score here. Then turn to page 211 and transfer your score onto Graph 1.

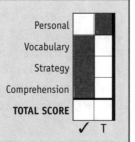

Check your answers with your teacher. Give yourself 1 point for each correct answer, and fill in your Vocabulary score here. Then turn to page 211 and transfer your score onto Graph 1.

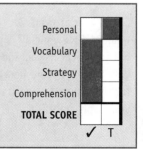

Strategy Check

Review the cause-and-effect chain you completed in the Strategy Follow-up. Also review the selection if necessary. Then answer these questions:

1. Why did Carol and Bill fall to their knees?
   a. They saw a small car.
   b. Lightning was falling all around them.
   c. They couldn't walk.

2. What did Carol and Bill do when they reached an abandoned car?
   a. They got into it until the storm passed.
   b. They drove to Carol's sister's house.
   c. They drove to the emergency room.

3. Why were Carol and Bill scared when they visited a museum?
   a. They were struck by lightning.
   b. They heard lightning in the distance.
   c. They saw a lightning demonstration.

4. At the museum, what did Carol and Bill do to find out what had happened to them?
   a. They stood behind a shield of grounded wires.
   b. They showed a scientist the burn marks on their feet.
   c. They talked to Carol's sister.

5. What happened to Bill and Carol when the lightning struck them?
   a. The lightning entered one foot and exited the other.
   b. The lightning missed them.
   c. The lightning struck their hearts and other organs.

Comprehension Check

Review the selection if necessary. Then answer these questions:

1. When did the author learn that Chicken Little is sometimes right?
   a. when she got caught in a lightning storm one summer evening
   b. when she felt an earthquake
   c. when softball-sized hail fell from the sky one summer evening

2. What happened as Carol and Bill tried to make their way out of the forest?
   a. A bomb exploded at Carol's feet.
   b. They were struck by lightning.
   c. They got lost.

3. Why couldn't Bill answer Carol when she called him?
   a. He was knocked unconscious by the lightning.
   b. He couldn't hear her because of all the loud thunder.
   c. The muscles around his mouth weren't working.

4. Why did Carol and Bill return to the forest the next day?
   a. They wanted to find out if they had dreamed the whole thing.
   b. They hoped to see something that would tell them what had happened to them.
   c. They wanted to look for Carol's car.

5. When Carol and Bill left the museum, why were they pinching and poking themselves once again?
   a. They were happier than ever to have survived the lightning strike.
   b. They were struck by lightning in the museum's lightning demonstration.
   c. Their bodies still felt numb and tingly from the strike a few days earlier.

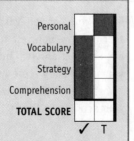

Check your answers with your teacher. Give yourself 1 point for each correct answer, and fill in your Strategy score here. Then turn to page 211 and transfer your score onto Graph 1.

Personal
Vocabulary
Strategy
Comprehension
TOTAL SCORE
✓ T

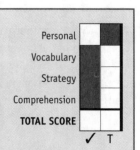

Check your answers with your teacher. Give yourself 1 point for each correct answer, and fill in your Comprehension score here. Then turn to page 211 and transfer your score onto Graph 1.

Personal
Vocabulary
Strategy
Comprehension
TOTAL SCORE
✓ T

Extending

Choose one or more of these activities:

REPORT THE WEATHER
Using the Internet or resources listed on this page, find out more about lightning and storms. Then, based on what you learned, write up a news report that warns people of a coming storm. Be sure to provide safety tips in your report. If you have time, videotape your weather report and share it with the class.

SKETCH A SCENE
Review "Lucky to Be Alive." Then choose a scene from the selection and illustrate it.

WRITE A PERSONAL ACCOUNT
Think about a frightening or thrilling experience that you have had. Tell what happened to you, and explain why those things happened. Then write a personal account of the events.

Resources

Books
Harper, Suzanne. *Lightning: Sheets, Streaks, Beads, and Balls.* Franklin Watts, 1997.

Simon, Seymour. *Lightning.* HarperTrophy, 1999.

———. *Storms.* HarperTrophy, 1992.

Web Sites
http://sln.fi.edu/weather/lightning/lightning.html
This Web site provides information on the history, science, and detection of lightning.

http://www.kidslightning.info/
This kid-friendly Web site contains information and stories about lightning strikes. It also provides tips on staying safe during a lightning storm.

http://www.mos.org/sln/toe/
This Web site provides information on electricity and lightning.

Video/DVD
Lightning. Nova: Adventures in Science. WGBH Boston Video, 1996.

LESSON 8 The Fitting-In of Kwan Su

Building Background

In the story you are about to read, Kwan Su is having trouble fitting in at her new school. Think about what you had to do to fit in at your school. What new rules did you have to learn? How did you make friends? What do you know now that you wish you knew then? Share your knowledge. On the lines below, write some advice that would help new students fit in at your school.

_____

_____

_____

beamed

dreaded

immature

obnoxious

suspiciously

uncoordinated

Vocabulary Builder

1. The words in the margin are from "The Fitting-In of Kwan Su." Do you know the meanings of these words? If not, making word trees can help you understand them. A word tree can include synonyms, or words that have the same meaning. It also can include examples and a definition of the word. Look at the following word tree for *famous*:

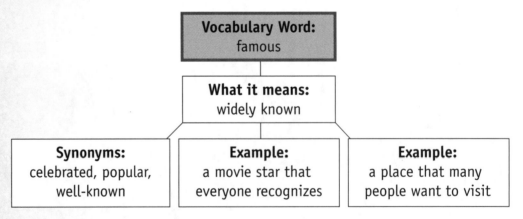

Vocabulary Word:
famous

What it means:
widely known

Synonyms:
celebrated, popular, well-known

Example:
a movie star that everyone recognizes

Example:
a place that many people want to visit

2. Start a word tree for each vocabulary word. (You will need to use your own paper.) Then, as you read "The Fitting-In of Kwan Su," fill in each tree with synonyms, examples, and a definition of the word. Use context clues to help you figure out each word's meaning. Or look it up in a dictionary.

3. Save your work. You will use it again in the Vocabulary Check.

Strategy Builder

Identifying Problems and Solutions

- In some stories, the main character or characters have a **problem**. Throughout the story, the characters try to solve the problem. Sometimes they try more than one **solution**. By the end of the story, they usually come up with a solution that works—the **end result**.

- As you read the following paragraphs, notice Gigi's problem and what she does to solve it. Do you think the end result is a good one? Why or why not?

> A week after tryouts, the cast of the spring play was posted on Mr. Valadez's door. Gigi had been given the starring role. Her stomach sank. A week ago she would have been thrilled. Right after tryouts, however, she'd joined the track team. How could she run track and manage the lead role in the play? As she studied the list, Gigi saw that a smaller part hadn't been assigned yet. "I know," she said to herself. "I'll talk to Mr. Valadez and tell him about the track team. I'll explain that I don't have enough time to play the lead, but that I could manage a small part. That way, I'll be able to run track and take part in the play."

- If you wanted to show the problem and solutions in the paragraph above, you could create a **problem-solution frame**. It would look something like this:

What is the problem?
Gigi joined the track team and got the lead role in the spring play.

Why is it a problem?
She doesn't have time to do both well.

Solutions	Results
1. Gigi studied the casting list.	1. She discovered that a small part had not been assigned yet.
2. She decided to talk to Mr. Valadez about taking a smaller part in the play.	2. **END RESULT:** If Mr. Valadez agrees, Gigi can run track and take part in the play.

The Fitting-In of Kwan Su

By Janet Gonter

As you read the first part of this story, notice Carla's problem. (It is circled.) Then notice the solutions she tries, and the results of each one. (Her solutions are underlined once. The results are underlined twice.) Why does Carla keep trying new solutions?

The first time I saw Kwan Su, I knew I had to help her. It was rather like the time I found a hurt, baby robin. Mom was upset with me for bringing it home, but a week later that baby robin flew away.

Kwan Su was small—really small to be 12. Her clothes were nice, but they were obviously little girls' clothing. The boys in my class acted **immature** as always.

"Hey, little girl," **obnoxious** Brant said, "kindergarten's down the hall." His friends laughed their heads off.

Kwan Su looked up with her huge brown eyes and then opened a book, pretending to read.

"Look! The book's upside down!" Brant laughed. The boys practically rolled on the floor.

A tear splashed on the open page.

I couldn't stand it anymore. "Come on, guys. Just grow up!"

A fight broke out in the hall, and off they raced.

I looked down at this tiny girl and promised myself that somehow I would help her. But how do you help someone that is so different fit in around here?

I sat down next to her. "Hi," I said quietly. All I knew was that her brother and she were orphans from Vietnam. They had just been adopted by a family in our town who decided that the best way for them to learn American ways was to be with American kids. I wasn't so sure.

She looked up at me with a question in her eyes. "My name is Carla," I said. "You're Kwan Su, right?"

Slowly, **suspiciously**, she nodded. "Kwan Su," she said.

Her schedule stuck out of one of her books. "May I see?" I asked. She had no idea what I meant. The schedule was pretty much the same as mine.

"Kwan Su," I said, "stick with me." I stood up and she did too.

Everywhere we went, kids pointed and stared. What was I doing to my own reputation? <u>I already felt like an unpopular geek. If I stuck with Kwan Su, I could really mess things up.</u> But then I imagined being suddenly placed into a Vietnamese school, not knowing the language and being a foot taller than everyone else, and being popular didn't seem nearly as important anymore. If you took the worst day of my whole life and multiplied it by a zillion, it couldn't have been nearly as bad as today must be for Kwan Su. How could I help her fit in? There had to be a way.

The talent show! <u>Maybe she could do something in the talent show.</u> As we went to music and gym, I soon realized that music and gymnastics were definitely not her strengths. She was almost as **uncoordinated** as me.

If Kwan Su were going to enter the talent show next month, she had to have a talent. But what?

Kwan Su was picking up English fast and understanding more and more of what I said. <u>But whenever I mentioned the talent show, she replied with her favorite American words, "No way!"</u>

Maybe it wasn't such a good idea after all.

 Stop here for the Strategy Break.

Strategy Break

If you were to create a problem-solution frame for the story so far, it might look like this:

What is the problem?
Carla wants to help Kwan Su fit in.

Why is it a problem?
Kwan Su is very different, so Carla isn't sure how to help her.

Solutions	Results
1. Carla tells Kwan Su to stick with her.	1. Carla worries about becoming more unpopular.
2. Carla thinks that Kwan Su could do something in the talent show.	2. Kwan Su says, "No way!"

As you continue reading, keep paying attention to what Carla does to try and solve the problem. Underline each solution once and each result twice. At the end of the story, you will create a problem-solution frame of your own.

Go on reading to see what happens.

Then one day, when I arrived at homeroom, Kwan Su was already there, making little pencil lines in her notebook.

"Hi!" I said.

"Hi, Calla," her version of Carla.

I happened to glance at her notebook, and I couldn't believe my eyes. She had opened her geography book to a picture of a train, and in her notebook, she had made a perfect copy.

"Kwan Su!" I said. "Where did you learn to draw like that?"

She shrugged like always when she didn't understand.

"The talent show," I said. "You can do that."

"No way!" She meant it.

Still, I took her to see the art teacher, Miss Palmer, and showed her what she had drawn.

"Why, it's wonderful," said Miss Palmer. "Listen," she said suddenly to Kwan Su. "Could you help me?"

Kwan Su looked at me and shrugged.

"She doesn't understand," I said. "Could you show her what you want?"

Miss Palmer showed me a poster she had painted for the talent show. "I need more of these, but I just don't have time. Do you think Kwan Su could help?"

"I'm sure of it!" I handed a bunch of posterboard and some acrylic paints to Kwan Su. Then I pointed to the little poster. "Make more?" I asked.

"Make more?" she repeated. "Make more?"

Suddenly she understood. "Yes," she **beamed**, "Kwan Su make many more!"

"Great," said Miss Palmer.

The day of the talent show finally arrived, and Kwan Su wasn't entered, but her posters were everywhere—all over the school and all over town, each one different.

Everyone loved the posters, but only Miss Palmer and I knew who'd painted them.

Kwan Su enjoyed the talent show. I'd never seen her smile so much. She had a nice smile.

"And finally," said Principal Brown, "we have a very special award."

Everyone wondered what was up.

"I'm sure you've all noticed the wonderful posters." Everyone nodded. "One of our very own students painted them." I could hear everyone whispering. Who could draw that well in our school?

Mr. Brown continued. "Since this student worked so hard on the posters, she deserves a prize too. Our mystery artist is our newest student—Kwan Su!"

When she heard her name, she looked scared to death. Everyone was looking at her. This was what she'd **dreaded** about the talent show: being stared at.

I squeezed her tiny hand. "He wants to give you a prize."

"P-P-Prize?" she asked with a shrug.

"A present."

Still, she looked terrified.

"I'll go with you." I pointed to us and the stage. Slowly, she nodded, and up we went.

Mr. Brown thanked Kwan Su for all the wonderful posters. Then he gave her something that made her very happy. It was a professional artist's set. Her face lit up. "M-M-Mine?" she asked.

He smiled kindly, "Yours."

"Oh, thank you," she cried. I realized at that moment she'd probably never owned anything in her whole life.

Everyone started to clap. She gave them a shy smile.

"Way to go, Kwan Su!" someone yelled. It was that obnoxious Brant. The applause was deafening.

Kwan Su beamed. Then I knew I'd saved another baby bird. Kwan Su was going to be all right. ●

Strategy Follow-up

Now create a problem-solution frame for the second part of "The Fitting-In of Kwan Su." For the problem box, use the information from the Strategy Break. Fill in the solution box with information from the second part of the story. Don't forget to label the end result.

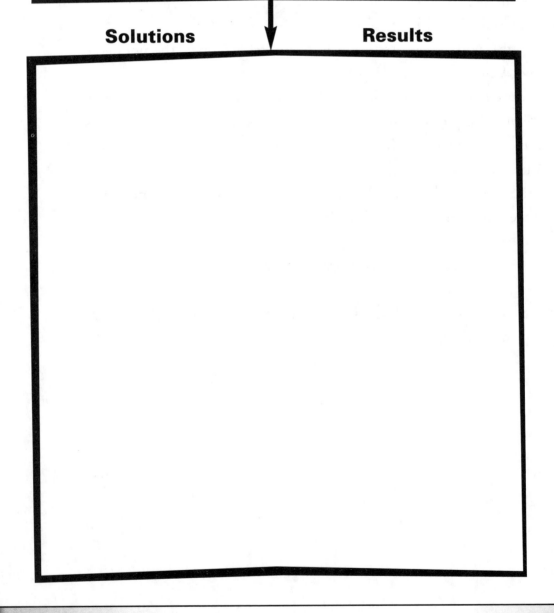

What is the problem?
Carla wants to help Kwan Su fit in.

Why is it a problem?
Kwan Su is very different, so Carla isn't sure how to help her.

Solutions   **Results**

✓Personal Checklist

Read each question and put a check (✓) in the correct box.

1. In Building Background, how well were you able to write some advice that would help new students fit in at your school?
   - ☐ 3 (extremely well)
   - ☐ 2 (fairly well)
   - ☐ 1 (not well)

2. In the Vocabulary Builder, how many word trees were you able to complete?
   - ☐ 3 (5–6 word trees)
   - ☐ 2 (3–4 word trees)
   - ☐ 1 (0–2 word trees)

3. How well were you able to identify the problems and solutions in the selection?
   - ☐ 3 (extremely well)
   - ☐ 2 (fairly well)
   - ☐ 1 (not well)

4. How well do you understand why Carla wants to help Kwan Su?
   - ☐ 3 (extremely well)
   - ☐ 2 (fairly well)
   - ☐ 1 (not well)

5. How well do you understand how Kwan Su feels after she gets a prize at the talent show?
   - ☐ 3 (extremely well)
   - ☐ 2 (fairly well)
   - ☐ 1 (not well)

Vocabulary Check

Look back at the work you did in the Vocabulary Builder. Then answer each question by circling the correct letter.

1. *Grinned* is a synonym of which vocabulary word?
   a. dreaded
   b. beamed
   c. uncoordinated

2. What could you list on a word tree as an example of obnoxious behavior?
   a. helping someone fit in
   b. laughing at someone who is different
   c. entering a talent show

3. What could you list on a word tree as a definition of *immature*?
   a. acting your age
   b. acting childishly
   c. acting like an adult

4. *Mistrustfully* is a synonym of which vocabulary word?
   a. immature
   b. obnoxious
   c. suspiciously

5. For which word could you list "thinking about an important test" as an example?
   a. dreaded
   b. beamed
   c. uncoordinated

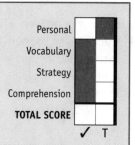

Add the numbers that you just checked to get your Personal Checklist score. Fill in your score here. Then turn to page 211 and transfer your score onto Graph 1.

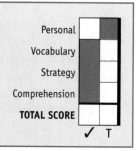

Check your answers with your teacher. Give yourself 1 point for each correct answer, and fill in your Vocabulary score here. Then turn to page 211 and transfer your score onto Graph 1.

Strategy Check

Review the problem-solution frame you completed in the Strategy Follow-up. Also review the selection if necessary. Then answer these questions:

1. What is the result of Carla's discovery that Kwan Su is a good artist?
   a. Kwan Su teaches Carla to paint.
   b. Carla encourages Kwan Su to enter her artwork in the talent show, and Kwan Su agrees.
   c. Carla encourages Kwan Su to enter her artwork in the talent show, but Kwan Su refuses.

2. What solution does Carla try after talking to Kwan Su about entering the talent show?
   a. Carla takes Kwan Su to Miss Palmer and shows her the girl's work.
   b. Carla encourages Kwan Su to join the gymnastics team.
   c. Carla teaches Kwan Su English.

3. What is the result of going to see the art teacher?
   a. Miss Palmer convinces Kwan Su to enter the talent contest.
   b. Miss Palmer asks Kwan Su to help her in class.
   c. Miss Palmer asks Kwan Su to make posters for the talent show.

4. What solution leads to the end result?
   a. Kwan Su and Carla walk up on the stage.
   b. Kwan Su paints many posters, which are displayed everywhere.
   c. Kwan Su enjoys the talent show.

5. What is the end result of the problem?
   a. Kwan Su receives a prize for her posters, and everyone applauds her.
   b. Kwan Su enters the talent show.
   c. Kwan Su becomes one of the most popular girls in her class.

Comprehension Check

Review the story if necessary. Then answer these questions:

1. Who is Kwan Su?
   a. She's a Vietnamese orphan who was adopted by a family in Carla's town.
   b. She is the daughter of a visiting Vietnamese official.
   c. She is a Vietnamese girl who came to town with her family.

2. Why do the boys at school tease Kwan Su at the beginning of the story?
   a. They tease her because she doesn't know how to write.
   b. They tease her because she is small and wears little girls' clothing.
   c. They tease her because her English is not very good.

3. Why does Carla decide to help Kwan Su?
   a. Carla wants to be popular.
   b. Carla used to live in Vietnam and can speak the language.
   c. Carla imagines herself in Kwan Su's place.

4. How does Carla find out that Kwan Su is a good artist?
   a. She sees a sketch in Kwan Su's notebook.
   b. Kwan Su tells her.
   c. The art teacher tells Carla about Kwan Su's talent.

5. At the end of the story, Carla says, "I knew I'd saved another baby bird. Kwan Su was going to be all right." What does Carla mean?
   a. Carla knows that Kwan Su will fit in now.
   b. Carla had saved another robin.
   c. Carla didn't want to be friends with Kwan Su anymore.

Check your answers with your teacher. Give yourself 1 point for each correct answer, and fill in your Strategy score here. Then turn to page 211 and transfer your score onto Graph 1.

Personal
Vocabulary
Strategy
Comprehension
TOTAL SCORE
✓ T

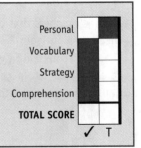

Check your answers with your teacher. Give yourself 1 point for each correct answer, and fill in your Comprehension score here. Then turn to page 211 and transfer your score onto Graph 1.

Personal
Vocabulary
Strategy
Comprehension
TOTAL SCORE
✓ T

Extending

Choose one or both of these activities:

LEARN ABOUT VIETNAM

Use the resources listed on this page to learn about Vietnam. In particular, find out about the Vietnamese who have immigrated to the United States. What hardships did they have to overcome to get here? Where do they live now? How well are they fitting in? Share your findings with your class.

CREATE A POSTER

Draw or paint a poster that would make people want to attend a talent show at your school. You might want to draw pictures of people performing. Or you might want to create a colorful design. Use posterboard and paint or markers to create your poster.

Resources

Books

Isaac, John (photographer), and Keith Elliot Greenberg. *Vietnam: The Boat People Search for a Home.* Children in Crisis. Blackbirch Marketing, 1996.

Matthews, Jo. *I Remember Vietnam.* Why We Left. Raintree/Steck Vaughn, 1994.

Whelan, Gloria. *Goodbye, Vietnam.* Random House, 1993.

Web Sites

http://www.artcontest.com/index.html
This Web site conducts a weekly art contest for kids.

http://www.mcps.k12.md.us/schools/springbrookhs/rights/VA/history.htm
This Web site provides a brief history of Vietnamese immigrants in the United States.

Say What?

Building Background

What do you know about dogs and cats? If you or someone you know has one of these animals for a pet, you probably know a lot. Even if you don't have a pet, you've probably seen or read enough about dogs and cats to know something about their behavior. In the article you are about to read, you will learn about how dogs and cats communicate. Get together with a partner and list three or four facts you know—or think you know—about how dogs and cats "talk." Then read "Say What?" and compare your ideas with the information in the article.

behaviorist

cringes

critter

dominant

pecking order

solitary

submissive

Vocabulary Builder

1. The words in the margin are from "Say What?" The words can be used to complete the sentences below. Before you begin reading the article, try to complete as many of the sentences as possible.

    a. Another word for *creature* is _____.

    b. A _____ studies how people or animals behave.

    c. _____ creatures live alone.

    d. _____ people like to control others.

    e. _____ people let themselves be pushed around.

    f. Fifth graders are lower on the _____ than seventh graders.

    g. My dog _____ when I scold him.

2. Find the words as you read the article. Use context clues to figure out any that are unfamiliar to you. If necessary, change or add to the answers you've already written.

3. Save your work. You will use it again in the Vocabulary Check.

Strategy Builder

Comparing and Contrasting While You Read

- Authors often compare and contrast things when they write. **Comparing** means telling how two or more things are alike. **Contrasting** means telling how two or more things are different.

- Suppose you wanted to compare and contrast German shepherds and dachshunds. You might use a **comparison chart** like this:

	German Shepherds	**Dachshunds**
Origin	Germany	Germany
Size	very large	very small
Shape	long legs, muscular body, pointed ears	short legs, long body, drooping ears
Coat	thick hair, usually brown or black	short hair, usually brown

Say What?

By Tracey Randinelli

As you read the first part of this selection, apply the strategies you just learned. Notice how the author compares and contrasts the ways in which dogs and cats communicate.

Carol Stark says she can tell when her dog Chauncey wants attention. Chauncey, a four-year-old golden retriever, will pick some trash out of a garbage can. "Then," says Carol, "she prances around the living room like she's saying, 'Look what I have.' She does it even though she knows she's not supposed to."

Carol isn't the only pet owner who believes her pet's actions communicate its feelings. There are whole books that describe the meaning of animal body language. They claim if the animal's tail is up, for example, the **critter** is showing a certain feeling. If its ears are down, it's showing a different feeling.

But can you really know for sure what your pets are telling you? Not all pet experts think so. Dr. Linda Goodloe is an animal **behaviorist** in New York City. According to Goodloe, animals' actions don't always speak louder than words.

For example, most people assume that when a dog's tail is up, it's in a friendly mood. But many dogs don't raise their tails that high to begin with. "If it's a dog that's a little more **submissive**," says Goodloe, "the tail may wag, but it may be a little lower. You can't say that the tail up means it's friendly. It often is, but not always."

Cats can also be misunderstood. Most people think a cat is happy when it purrs. Cats *do* purr when they're content. But they may also purr when they're in pain.

And like people, animals may feel more than one emotion at a time. "A dog may be curious and want to greet you, but also a little fearful," says Goodloe. "Even if its tail is wagging, you could get bitten. You have to look at the situation and the individual dog."

 Stop here for the Strategy Break.

Strategy Break

If you were to make a comparison chart for the selection so far, it might look like this:

	Dogs	Cats
Happy	raise tail	purr
Fearful or in Pain	lower tail; might wag tail	purr

As you continue reading, keep looking for the ways in which dogs and cats are alike and different.

 Go on reading.

Getting Emotional

Many pet owners are certain their pet can tell how they're feeling, too. "If I'm sad," Carol says, "Chauncey comes over to me and looks into my eyes as if to say, 'It's okay.'"

But according to Goodloe, pets don't have the ability to pick up on our emotions as much as we think. That's because animals aren't able to show the kinds of emotions people have. "People seem to need to believe that this mental connection exists," Goodloe says. "But the person may be reading something in the behavior that isn't there."

In fact, your pet may not treat you much differently than it would another human—or another dog or cat. "Dogs that want to play do a bow with their front paws down," says Goodloe. "They'll do that with a cat, with a human or with another dog. If cats are feeling comfortable, they'll greet you with their tail in the air and rub against you. They'll do that to anyone if they feel that comfort level."

Carol has seen that kind of behavior in Chauncey. "If I go toward her on all fours and put my head down," she says, "she'll play rougher, like she's playing with another dog."

All in the Past

To understand how your pet communicates, it helps to know something about its ancestors. Take dogs. They are related to wolves. Wolves hunt and hang out in packs. In a group, wolves have a **pecking order**. Wolves let themselves be pushed around by a more **dominant** wolf.

Dogs act a lot like wolves. They like to be part of a family—including your family. If your dog howls when you leave it alone, it isn't necessarily feeling sad that you're not there. It may be saying, "I've been separated from the pack. I have to howl to let them know where I am."

A dog also accepts its owner as "top dog." Much of what it communicates is that you are boss. This is usually why a dog won't meet its master's eyes and why it rolls over and shows its belly, swallows or **cringes**.

Pack animals have to be able to get their point across to others in their group. That's why dogs are very expressive. Cats, on the other hand, are more **solitary**. They don't have the same large "vocabulary" as dogs. That means they're harder to figure out.

So how do you communicate with your pet? The best way is to remember it's an animal—not a small human friend. "Learn how animals look at the world," advises Dr. Goodloe. "They don't see or hear the same things." When you see things through your pet's eyes, you'll really understand what it's saying. ●

Strategy Follow-up

Now fill in this comparison chart for the second part of "Say What?" Go back and skim the selection for information when you need to.

	Dogs	Cats
How They Like to Live		
How They Show Playfulness or That They Are Comfortable		
How They Express Themselves		
How They Say, "You're the Boss"		

✓Personal Checklist

Read each question and put a check (✓) in the correct box.

1. In Building Background, how well were you able to list what you know about how dogs and cats communicate?
   - ☐ 3 (extremely well)
   - ☐ 2 (fairly well)
   - ☐ 1 (not well)

2. In the Vocabulary Builder, how many sentences did you complete correctly?
   - ☐ 3 (6–7 sentences)
   - ☐ 2 (3–5 sentences)
   - ☐ 1 (0–2 sentence)

3. How well were you able to compare and contrast dogs and cats in the Strategy Follow-up?
   - ☐ 3 (extremely well)
   - ☐ 2 (fairly well)
   - ☐ 1 (not well)

4. How well do you understand why dogs enjoy living with families?
   - ☐ 3 (extremely well)
   - ☐ 2 (fairly well)
   - ☐ 1 (not well)

5. How well do you understand why people believe that their pets show emotion?
   - ☐ 3 (extremely well)
   - ☐ 2 (fairly well)
   - ☐ 1 (not well)

Vocabulary Check

Look back at the work you did in the Vocabulary Builder. Then answer each question by circling the correct letter.

1. Which vocabulary word means the same thing as *alone*?
   - a. critter
   - b. solitary
   - c. dominant

2. Which vocabulary word is an antonym of *dominant*?
   - a. solitary
   - b. submissive
   - c. behaviorist

3. In a group, wolves have a pecking order. What does this mean?
   - a. The stronger wolves control the weaker wolves.
   - b. The wolves take turns biting each other.
   - c. The wolves take turns looking for food.

4. How does a dog show that its owner is boss?
   - a. The dog bows before its owner.
   - b. The dog rubs against its owner.
   - c. The dog cringes before its owner.

5. According to the article, what do animal behaviorists do?
   - a. They help sick and injured animals.
   - b. They study animals' actions.
   - c. They train dogs to do tricks.

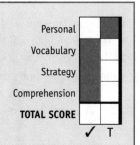

Add the numbers that you just checked to get your Personal Checklist score. Fill in your score here. Then turn to page 211 and transfer your score onto Graph 1.

Personal
Vocabulary
Strategy
Comprehension

TOTAL SCORE ✓ T

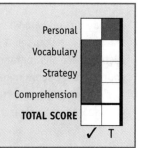

Check your answers with your teacher. Give yourself 1 point for each correct answer, and fill in your Vocabulary score here. Then turn to page 211 and transfer your score onto Graph 1.

Personal
Vocabulary
Strategy
Comprehension

TOTAL SCORE ✓ T

Strategy Check

Review the comparison chart you completed in the Strategy Follow-up. Also review the selection if necessary. Then answer these questions:

1. What is different about how dogs and cats live?

   a. Dogs like to live with wolves, and cats like to live with families.

   b. Dogs like to live alone, and cats like to live in groups.

   c. Dogs like to live in groups, and cats like to live alone.

2. Why are cats harder to figure out than dogs?

   a. They howl when their owners leave them alone.

   b. They aren't very expressive.

   c. They have a larger vocabulary than dogs.

3. What does the article say a dog does when it wants to play?

   a. It jumps up and plants its paws on its owner's chest.

   b. It rolls over onto its back.

   c. It bows with its front paws down.

4. What is a cat saying when it holds its tail up and rubs against you?

   a. The cat is saying that it is afraid.

   b. The cat is saying that it feels comfortable.

   c. The cat is saying that it is in pain.

5. A dog may roll over and show its belly when it's being submissive. According to the article, how does a cat show that you're the boss?

   a. It cringes.

   b. It swallows.

   c. Neither answer is correct.

Comprehension Check

Review the article if necessary. Then answer these questions:

1. According to the article, what do many pet owners believe?

   a. that their dogs like to eat garbage

   b. that dogs are sweeter than cats

   c. that their pets can communicate feelings

2. Which of the following is *least* likely to happen if you pet a dog whose tail is wagging?

   a. The dog will bite you.

   b. The dog will ignore you.

   c. The dog will lick your hand.

3. When a cat is feeling comfortable, who does it rub against?

   a. any human

   b. only its owner

   c. a dog

4. Why do dogs like to be part of a family?

   a. Dogs are related to wolves, which are pack animals.

   b. Dogs are solitary animals.

   c. Dogs are very emotional.

5. What's the best way to communicate with a pet?

   a. Imagine that the pet feels what you feel.

   b. Try to see things through the pet's eyes.

   c. Get down on all fours and pretend to be a dog or cat.

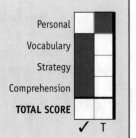

Check your answers with your teacher. Give yourself 1 point for each correct answer, and fill in your Strategy score here. Then turn to page 211 and transfer your score onto Graph 1.

Personal
Vocabulary
Strategy
Comprehension
TOTAL SCORE
✓ T

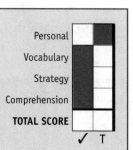

Check your answers with your teacher. Give yourself 1 point for each correct answer, and fill in your Comprehension score here. Then turn to page 211 and transfer your score onto Graph 1.

Personal
Vocabulary
Strategy
Comprehension
TOTAL SCORE
✓ T

Extending

Choose one or both of these activities:

ILLUSTRATE ANIMAL BEHAVIOR
Illustrate the behavior described in the article. You might draw a picture of a cat rubbing against someone's legs. Or you might draw a dog bowing, ready to play.

OBSERVE AN ANIMAL
Observe your own pet or one belonging to a friend. If the pet is a dog, notice when it wags its tail, bows, or cringes. If the pet is a cat, notice when it rubs against something or walks away. What emotions, if any, do you think the pet is expressing? Use the selection you just read and the resources listed on this page to read the animal's behavior.

Resources

Books

Ames, Lee J. *Draw 50 Animals.* Books for Young Readers. Main Street Books, 1985.

Fogle, Bruce. *The Cat's Mind: Understanding Your Cat's Behavior.* Hungry Minds, 1995.

Fogle, Bruce, and Anne B. Wilson. *The Dog's Mind: Understanding Your Dog's Behavior.* Howell, 1992.

Zalme, Ron. *How to Draw Puppies and Kittens.* Troll, 1999.

Web Site

http://www.avma.org/care4pets/
This Web site of the American Veterinary Medical Association provides information on pet health and animal safety. It has a link to a "Kid's corner" that contains animal-care activities for children.

Fire!

build

burned

destroy

die

end

ongoing

scatter

scorched

shoot up

spreads

sprout

survive

Building Background

The selection you are about to read tells what happens during a forest-fire cycle. A cycle is a sequence of events that repeat themselves over and over. For example, the seasons of the year follow an annual cycle. The year starts with spring, when plants and new growth begin. Spring is followed by summer, when things grow to adult size. In autumn, growth begins to die back. By winter, most plants have disappeared. Then in the spring, the cycle begins all over again.

The events in a cycle can be represented in a circle. As you read this selection, record the events in a forest-fire cycle in the circle below. The circle will help you see how the cycle repeats itself.

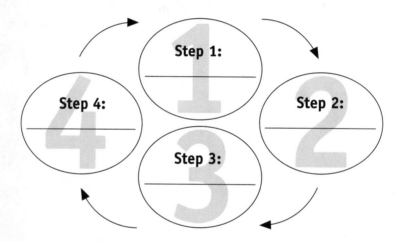

Step 1:

Step 2:

Step 3:

Step 4:

Vocabulary Builder

1. Study the vocabulary words in the margin. Each word is half of a pair of antonyms (words with opposite meanings) or synonyms (words with the same meaning).

2. Write the antonym pairs on Clipboard #1.

3. Write the synonym pairs on Clipboard #2.

4. As you read this selection, underline any other antonym or synonym pairs that you find.

5. Save your work. You will use it again in the Vocabulary Check.

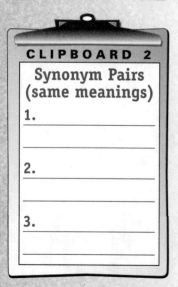

CLIPBOARD 1

Antonym Pairs (opposites)

1. _____

2. _____

3. _____

CLIPBOARD 2

Synonym Pairs (same meanings)

1. _____

2. _____

3. _____

Strategy Builder

Outlining Main Ideas and Supporting Details

- You already know that most informational writing describes a particular **topic**, such as buildings or lighthouses.

- You also know that most informational writing is organized according to **main ideas** and **supporting details**. These ideas and details help explain or support the topic.

- There are many ways to keep track of main ideas and details as you read. One way is to make a simple **outline**. Outlines can be helpful as you do research, plan your own writing, or study for a test.

- Some outlines use a system of Roman numerals (I, II, II, IV, V, and so on) and capital letters (A, B, C, D, E, and so on).

- Read the following paragraphs, which tell about the 1911 fire at the Triangle Shirtwaist Factory. Then read the outline of the paragraphs. Note how the main ideas are identified with Roman numerals, and the supporting details are shown with capital letters.

Triangle Shirtwaist Factory Fire

The working conditions at the factory led to a deadly fire on March 25, 1911. Once the fire broke out, it spread quickly, fed by the oil-soaked machines and piles of cloth. When the women workers tried to escape, they discovered that all but one of the exit doors were locked.

Anger over the fire—which resulted in 146 deaths—helped bring about changes. Stricter fire codes and a 54-hour work week for women and minors were established. A new child-labor law outlawing work for children under 14 was also passed.

Triangle Shirtwaist Factory Fire

I. Working conditions
   A. Oil-soaked machines
   B. Piles of cloth
   C. All but one exit door locked

II. Changes brought about by fire
   A. Stricter fire codes
   B. A 54-hour work week for women and children
   C. New child-labor law passed

Fire!

by Caroline Evans

As you read the first part of "Fire!" notice how it is organized. Think about how you might show the main ideas and supporting details in an outline.

Wild flames can turn a full-grown forest into a heap of ashes. Total destruction? Or a clean, new beginning?

Imagine a hot summer day in a forest in the western United States. A mighty thunderstorm turns the blue sky black. *Zap!* A bolt of lightning streaks toward the ground and strikes the top of a tall pine tree. Electric current zips down through its trunk and roots. In an instant, the pine tree explodes into a flaming torch.

The burning branches pop and **scatter** onto the forest floor. Fire **spreads** to dry twigs and needles. Flames dance over dead logs and leap up nearby tree trunks. Soon the forest crackles and snaps in a red-orange light.

This is the **end** of the forest, right? Actually, the answer is bigger than that. A fire can be just another step in the forest's **ongoing** natural cycle.

Step One: Beginning the Cycle

The forest-fire cycle has been happening over and over for thousands of years. Fire may seem to be terribly destructive, but many forests depend on it to stay healthy. Here's how it works in a western pine forest:

When the forest burns, the fire acts sort of like a giant gardener. It clears, trims, weeds—and even spreads seeds! Fire cleans up old leaves, needles, and dried-out logs and limbs heaped all over the ground. As this stuff burns, it turns into powdery ashes full of minerals. The minerals help new trees grow.

But where do the new trees come from? In a pine forest, they come from the seeds that grow in pine cones high up on branches. These cones are sealed in a sappy wrapping. When they get heated by fire, the sap melts and the cones burst open like popcorn. The seeds sail out in all directions, and some may land in ash-covered soil where the fire has already passed.

Burning Out

Forest fires usually start during the summer and may continue burning for several months before going out. A fire naturally goes out in one of two ways. It can run out of fuel (fallen wood and standing trees). Or it can be put out by rain or snow.

 Stop here for the Strategy Break.

Strategy Break

If you were to outline the main ideas and supporting details in "Fire!" so far, your outline might look like this:

I. Step One: Beginning the cycle
   A. A fire begins.
   B. The fire clears, trims, and spreads seeds.
   C. Minerals from the burned material help new trees grow.
   D. After several months, the fire goes out.

As you continue reading, keep paying attention to the main ideas and supporting details. At the end of this selection, you use some of them to complete an outline of your own.

 Go on reading.

Step Two: New Growth

Once the fire is out, the next step in the cycle begins. When spring comes, rainwater and melted snow help seeds **sprout**. Green grasses peep out of the black earth. In early summer, golden glacier lilies may pop up. Little pine seedlings sprout long, soft needles. And in late summer, fields of pink fireweed blossoms may spread throughout the area.

During this step of the cycle, animals may also benefit from the fire's work. Although some have lost their homes and hiding places, many animals can find new ones in burned-out tree trunks. They also can chow down on **scorched** bark and the new green growth that starts cropping up all around.

Newcomers Settle In

After a fire, lots of newcomers venture onto the scene. New trees and shrubs **shoot up** fast because more sunlight reaches the forest floor than before. Beetles chew into fallen trees and blackened logs. Woodpeckers and other birds **build** nests in burned-out tree holes.

The birds eat berries and leaves from newly grown woody plants. They also eat grasshoppers, ants, beetles, and caterpillars that find new homes in the **burned** woods.

A fire may **destroy** the usual nesting places of birds and other animals. But after a fire the forest is full of new nest sites to choose from. A pair of owls, for example, may pick a newly burned-out tree trunk to make a home for their owlets.

Step Three: Full of Life

The third step in the fire cycle is a healthy forest—filled with lots of different kinds of plants and animals. Seedlings grow into adult pines. During this time, many generations of animals are born, find mates, raise families, and **die** in the forest community.

Final Step: Old Age

If a fire doesn't happen sooner, a pine forest may **survive** for 200 to 300 years. But time begins to catch up with a forest that old. Some of the huge, aging pines begin to die. One wobbles and leans on the next. Another creaks, cracks, and crashes to the ground. Soon, many old giants lie scattered on the forest floor.

Then, on another summer day, black clouds darken the sky. Boom— *zap!* The fire cycle starts all over again. . . . ●

Strategy Follow-up

Now create an outline for Step Two in the forest-fire cycle. This step will be your outline's main idea. Parts of the details have been filled in for you.

II. Step Two: _____

  A. When spring comes, _____ .

  B. _____ , seedlings sprout.

  C. In late summer, _____ .

  D. Animals feed _____ and find

     _____ .

  E. New trees and shrubs _____ .

  F. Birds eat berries and bugs and _____ .

✓Personal Checklist

Read each question and put a check (✓) in the correct box.

1. In Building Background, how well were you able to record the forest-fire cycle on the circle?
   - ☐ 3 (extremely well)
   - ☐ 2 (fairly well)
   - ☐ 1 (not well)

2. In the Vocabulary Builder, how many synonym and antonym pairs were you able to identify?
   - ☐ 3 (5–6 pairs)
   - ☐ 2 (3–4 pairs)
   - ☐ 1 (0–2 pairs)

3. How well were you able to outline the main ideas and supporting details in the Strategy Follow-up?
   - ☐ 3 (extremely well)
   - ☐ 2 (fairly well)
   - ☐ 1 (not well)

4. How well do you understand the forest-fire cycle?
   - ☐ 3 (extremely well)
   - ☐ 2 (fairly well)
   - ☐ 1 (not well)

5. How well do you understand how a natural fire can be beneficial?
   - ☐ 3 (extremely well)
   - ☐ 2 (fairly well)
   - ☐ 1 (not well)

Vocabulary Check

Look back at the work you did in the Vocabulary Builder. Then answer each question by circling the correct letter.

1. Which word is an antonym of *build*?
   - a. survive
   - b. destroy
   - c. burned

2. Which word is a synonym of *scatter*?
   - a. sprout
   - b. shoot up
   - c. spread

3. After a fire, some animals chew on the scorched bark. What does *scorched* mean?
   - a. burned
   - b. dead
   - c. destroyed

4. The forest-fire cycle is ongoing. Which word is the opposite of *ongoing*?
   - a. survive
   - b. end
   - c. build

5. New plants shoot up after a fire because sunlight can reach the forest floor. What's another word for *shoot up*?
   - a. die
   - b. scatter
   - c. sprout

Add the numbers that you just checked to get your Personal Checklist score. Fill in your score here. Then turn to page 211 and transfer your score onto Graph 1.
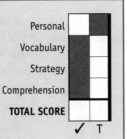

Check your answers with your teacher. Give yourself 1 point for each correct answer, and fill in your Vocabulary score here. Then turn to page 211 and transfer your score onto Graph 1.
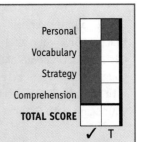

Strategy Check

Review the outline you completed in the Strategy Follow-up. Also review the selection if necessary. Then answer these questions:

1. What happens when spring comes to the forest?
   a. The fire continues burning.
   b. Seeds sprout.
   c. Pine trees begin to die.

2. How do animals and birds benefit from the fire's work?
   a. They die.
   b. They leave the forest.
   c. They eat the new growth and build new homes.

3. If you created an outline for Step Three of the cycle, which of the following might you list as the main idea?
   a. Step Three: Adult Forest
   b. Step Three: Old Age
   c. Step Three: Newcomers Settle In

4. If you created an outline for Step Three of the cycle, which of the following could you include as a supporting detail?
   a. Seedlings grow into adult pines.
   b. The fire cycle starts all over again.
   c. New trees and shrubs shoot up.

5. If you created an outline for the final step of the cycle, which of the following could you include as a supporting detail?
   a. The forest is filled with healthy plants.
   b. Some of the aging pines begin to die.
   c. The fire is put out by rain or snow.

Comprehension Check

Review the article if necessary. Then answer these questions:

1. According to the article, how might a forest fire start naturally?
   a. The hot sun beats down on dry leaves until they burst into flames.
   b. A bolt of lightning strikes a tree, and it explodes into a flaming torch.
   c. A careless person doesn't put out a campfire.

2. How long has the forest-fire cycle been happening?
   a. It's been happening over and over for thousands of years.
   b. It's been happening for 200 or 300 years.
   c. It's been happening for about ten years.

3. After a fire has burned a forest to ashes, how do new pine trees get started?
   a. Volunteers come into the area and plant seedlings.
   b. The ashes contain seeds.
   c. Heated pine cones burst open, and their seeds scatter on the forest floor.

4. During the third step of the cycle, how many generations of animals live and die in the forest community?
   a. one generation
   b. two generations
   c. many generations

5. In the final step of the cycle, what happens when aging pines begin to die?
   a. They grow into adult pines.
   b. They fall to the forest floor.
   c. They are set on fire.

Check your answers with your teacher. Give yourself 1 point for each correct answer, and fill in your Strategy score here. Then turn to page 211 and transfer your score onto Graph 1.

Personal
Vocabulary
Strategy
Comprehension
TOTAL SCORE
✓ T

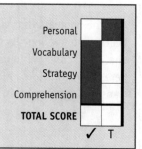

Check your answers with your teacher. Give yourself 1 point for each correct answer, and fill in your Comprehension score here. Then turn to page 211 and transfer your score onto Graph 1.

Personal
Vocabulary
Strategy
Comprehension
TOTAL SCORE
✓ T

Extending

Choose one or more of these activities:

COMPLETE THE OUTLINE
Create outlines for the last two steps described in the article. List the main ideas and supporting details in the steps.

ILLUSTRATE THE FIRE CYCLE
Illustrate the fire cycle using the information in the article. When you have finished, display your illustration in your classroom. Can your classmates follow the order of events and understand what happens at each stage of the cycle?

RESEARCH FOREST FIRES
Work alone or with a group to find out more about forest fires. One specific topic you might consider is how firefighters deal with and control forest fires that start naturally. Do they let the fires run their course? Do they try to put the fires out? Use the resources listed on this page. Report your findings orally or in writing.

Resources

Books
Lampton, Christopher F. *Forest Fire.* Disaster! Millbrook Press, 1991.

Patent, Dorothy Hinshaw. *Fire: Friend or Foe?* Clarion Books, 1998.

———. *Yellowstone Fires: Flames and Rebirth.* Holiday House, 1990.

Web Site
http://www.smokeybear.com/only_you_html.asp
This Web site explains the science of wildfires and provides information on preventing and fighting forest fires.

Learning New Words

VOCABULARY

From Lesson 8
- uncoordinated

Prefixes

A prefix is a word part that is added to the beginning of a root word. For example, the prefix *pre-* means "before," so adding *pre-* to the root word *view* makes it a verb meaning "view before."

un-

The prefix *un-* means "not." In "The Fitting-in of Kwan Su" you learned that someone who is *uncoordinated* is not coordinated, or does not move smoothly. Notice that adding this prefix does not change the part of speech.

    Now write the word that means the same as the phrases below.

1. not willing   _____

2. not able   _____

3. not known   _____

4. not written   _____

5. not paid   _____

From Lesson 8
- immature

im-

The prefix *im-* also means "not." In "The Fitting-In of Kwan Su" you learned that someone who is *immature* is not mature, or does not act grown-up. As with *un-*, adding the prefix *im-* does not change the part of speech.

    Now write the definition of each word below.

1. impossible   _____

2. immeasurable   _____

3. immobile   _____

4. immortal   _____

5. impractical   _____

Multiple-Meaning Words

VOCABULARY

From Lesson 7
- current
- film
- limbs
- shaken
- skirt
- strained

A single word can have more than one meaning. For example, the word *current* can mean "up-to-date" or "electrical flow." To figure out which meaning of *current* an author is using, you have to use context. Context is the information surrounding a word or situation that helps you understand its meaning.

When you read "Lucky to Be Alive" you used context to figure out that the author uses *current* to mean "electrical flow."

Use context to figure out the correct meaning of each underlined word. Circle the letter of the correct meaning.

1. Everything was covered with a delicate <u>film</u> of dust.

   a. material on which movies and photographs are made

   b. thin coating or layer

2. The army <u>skirted</u> the area where the battle had been.

   a. ran along the edge of

   b. avoided or ignored

3. The ground was covered with <u>limbs</u> and leaves after the storm.

   a. arms and legs

   b. tree branches

4. Babies often eat <u>strained</u> peas.

   a. exerted to the limit

   b. with lumps removed

5. I was quite <u>shaken</u> by the dog's attack.

   a. moved back and forth rapidly

   b. emotionally upset

Damon and Pythias

Building Background

The story you are about to read is a legend. A **legend** is a story that has been passed down from generation to generation. Legends are not true, but they are usually based on real people or events. The stories often exaggerate the heroes' good qualities. For example, you've probably heard the legend about the young George Washington, in which he confesses to chopping down a cherry tree. The story isn't true, but it exaggerates Washington's commonly accepted honesty. Get together with a partner and share the legends you know. You might share legends about presidents, such as George Washington or Abraham Lincoln. Or you might discuss such legendary American heroes as Johnny Appleseed, John Henry, or Davy Crockett.

beset

decreed

defied

forfeit

heedless

meager

mercenaries

sought

treason

tyrant

Vocabulary Builder

1. Each of the sentences below contains a **boldfaced** vocabulary word. As you read each sentence, first use context clues to figure out what the boldfaced word means. Then decide whether it is used correctly or not.

2. If the boldfaced word is used correctly, write a **C** on the line. If it is not used correctly, write an **I** on the line.

_____ a. We were **beset** by thieves, who robbed and beat us.

_____ b. When the law was **decreed**, we knew it didn't have to be obeyed.

_____ c. The man **defied** his leader when he did exactly what she ordered.

_____ d. She will not lose her life because her life is **forfeit**.

_____ e. He was **heedless** of the danger; he didn't care what might happen.

_____ f. Sara's **meager** belongings filled boxes and boxes.

_____ g. The **mercenaries** were paid to fight the attacking army.

_____ h. Juan **sought** his missing dog but couldn't find it.

_____ i. They commited **treason** by remaining loyal to their country.

_____ j. The **tyrant** was a kind ruler who listened to his people.

3. Save your work. You will use it again in the Vocabulary Check.

Strategy Builder

Making Predictions While Reading a Story

- When you read a story, you probably try to **predict**, or guess, what will happen next. Like a detective, you use clues to help you make your predictions.

- The clues in a story are sometimes called its context. Remember that **context** is information that comes before or after a word or situation to help you understand it better.

- As you read "Damon and Pythias," you will stop twice to make predictions. At each Strategy Break, you will write down which context clues helped you make your predictions. Then, after you finish reading the story, you will look back at your predictions and see which ones match what actually happened.

Damon and Pythias

A Greek legend adapted by Teresa Bateman

See if you can use the clues that the author provides to predict what will happen to Damon and Pythias.

Dionysius was a **tyrant**. Everyone in Sicily agreed on that. He ruled with an iron hand and was little loved and much feared. Still, there were those who **sought** his favor—hangers-on who told Dionysius only what he wished to hear. He enjoyed their words but trusted no one.

Dionysius had a bodyguard of a thousand men—soldiers, **mercenaries**, and slaves. The tyrant made his home in Syracuse, on a small isthmus separated from the mainland by a wall with five gates through which every visitor had to pass. He locked his room at night and slept on a bed surrounded by a small moat to which he alone controlled the drawbridge. Thus he thought to protect himself from all who sought his life.

The Tyrant of Syracuse had no mercy for anyone who **defied** him. He knew little of love and nothing of friendship.

In the town of Syracuse there lived two young men named Damon and Pythias. They had studied together for many years and were the closest of friends. Indeed, the townspeople knew that to find one was to find the other, for they were rarely apart.

One day Pythias gave a speech in the marketplace, defying Dionysius and questioning his right to rule. He did not think about the consequences, only that he must speak the truth.

Suddenly the bodyguards of Dionysius filled the square.

"Run!" the people shouted. "Hide!"

But it was too late. The guards carried Pythias away to be sentenced for **treason**. The townspeople fled before the marching men—all but Damon who, **heedless** of the risk, followed after his friend. Silent as a shadow he slipped through the five gates and found a place in the courtyard where he could learn his friend's fate.

 Stop here for Strategy Break #1.

Strategy Break #1

1. What do you predict will happen next?

_____

_____

2. Why do you think so?

_____

_____

3. What clues from the story helped you make your prediction(s)?

_____

_____

_____

 Go on reading to see what happens.

"Kneel," demanded Dionysius as Pythias was brought before him. But the young man refused.

"I bow only to my betters," he said.

Damon watched in horror as Dionysius's face grew red with anger.

"So, I am no better than a peasant?" the ruler shouted. "You doubt my power? Let me demonstrate it. I hereby sentence you to death." He turned to the guards. "Take him to prison to await his execution!"

Pythias paled at the judgment but stood his ground.

"If I am to die for my beliefs, so be it," he said calmly. "Yet I would ask a favor. My parents are not young. Allow me to return home and set my **meager** affairs in order so that they may be cared for in their old age. I will return in a month's time, and then you may carry out your judgment."

Dionysius laughed. "Do I look a fool? If you leave this courtyard with a sentence of death, you will never return. You will run for the rest of your days to escape my judgment."

Pythias gazed long at the ruler. "I give you the word of an honest man," he said simply.

"There are no honest men when life or death is the prize," Dionysius declared.

Then Damon stepped forth from the crowd.

"Not true," Damon said. "I know of at least two honest men—myself and my friend. Set Pythias free to settle his affairs, and I will take his place in prison."

"Then you are a fool," Dionysius said. "What guarantee have you that he will return?"

Damon placed a hand on his friend's shoulder. "I need no guarantee," he said. "He is my friend. I know him like a brother. Pythias will keep his word."

"And if he does not?" Dionysius pressed on.

"Then I will die in his place," Damon replied.

The Tyrant of Syracuse was taken aback by the friendship of the two young men. He decided to put it to the test.

"Very well," he agreed. "But if Pythias does not return in one month, I will not spare Damon from the punishment I have **decreed**. One of you shall die."

Pythias embraced Damon. "Thank you, my friend," he said. "I will return as quickly as I can. Trust in me."

"I always have," Damon replied as the guards carried him away to prison.

 Stop here for Strategy Break #2.

Strategy Break #2

1. Do your earlier predictions match what happened? _____ Why or why not?

_____

_____

2. What do you predict will happen next?

_____

_____

3. Why do you think so?

_____

_____

4. What clues from the tale helped you make your prediction(s)?

_____

_____

 Go on reading to see what happens.

Pythias ran from the courtyard, anxious to put his affairs in order so that he could return in good time to save his friend.

Days went by, and as each passed, Dionysius visited the prison, hoping to see Damon lose faith. To his surprise, the young man stood firm.

"Pythias will return," Damon said. "I have no doubt of it."

More days went by. The other prisoners began to mock Damon. "You were a fool to trust your friend," they said. "No man can be trusted when his life would be **forfeit**."

But Damon's faith was unshakable.

Days turned to weeks. A month was what Dionysius had given Pythias, no more, and that month was drawing to a close.

"What of your friend now?" Dionysius asked on one of his visits to the prison. "He has abandoned you to his fate."

"He has been delayed," Damon insisted. "He has met with trouble along the way, but I have nothing to fear. He will return, and in time."

At last the day of the execution dawned. The prisoner was brought before the Tyrant of Syracuse to meet his death.

"What say you now?" asked Dionysius. "You have been abandoned and must face a death you have not earned. Do you still believe in Pythias?"

"I do," Damon stated. "If he is not here, it is because something has happened to prevent him. So be it. I will gladly give my life for my friend."

"Bring the executioner," ordered the ruler, made uneasy by the young man's words.

Damon knelt before Dionysius, prepared to meet his fate.

Just then there was a disturbance in the outer courtyard, and a ragged figure ran through the gates. He staggered forward and threw himself down beside Damon. Weeping, he embraced him.

"I am in time! Thank the gods I am in time!"

It was Pythias.

"I set about my business quickly," Pythias explained, panting with exhaustion. "I was hurrying back when robbers **beset** me, beating me and taking what little I had. When I regained my senses, many days had passed. I have been running ever since, fearing I would be too late. Thank the gods I am in time to save my friend!"

"I knew you would come," Damon replied.

Pythias turned to Dionysius. "I am ready to receive my punishment," he said. "Free my friend."

There was a long silence. Dionysius had a strange look on his face, like that of a thirsty man who can hear and see a rushing stream but has not the strength to reach it.

"I revoke the sentence of death," he said at last. "The world cannot afford to lose honest men who know the meaning of friendship. Although I live in a crowd, I now realize that I am painfully alone. You both are free to go, but could you grant me one favor first?"

The young men stood together, facing the ruler.

"Might I be the third in your friendship?" Dionysius asked humbly. ●

Strategy Follow-up

Go back and look at the predictions that you wrote in this lesson. Do any of them match what actually happened in this story? Why or why not?

✓Personal Checklist

Read each question and put a check (✓) in the correct box.

1. In Building Background, how well were you able to share the legends that you are familiar with?
   - ☐ 3 (extremely well)
   - ☐ 2 (fairly well)
   - ☐ 1 (not well)

2. In the Vocabulary Builder, how well were you able to figure out if the boldfaced words were used correctly?
   - ☐ 3 (extremely well)
   - ☐ 2 (fairly well)
   - ☐ 1 (not well)

3. How well do you understand why Damon trusts Pythias?
   - ☐ 3 (extremely well)
   - ☐ 2 (fairly well)
   - ☐ 1 (not well)

4. How well do you understand Dionysius's final judgment?
   - ☐ 3 (extremely well)
   - ☐ 2 (fairly well)
   - ☐ 1 (not well)

5. How well were you able to predict what might happen next in the story?
   - ☐ 3 (extremely well)
   - ☐ 2 (fairly well)
   - ☐ 1 (not well)

Vocabulary Check

Look back at the work you did in the Vocabulary Builder. Then answer each question by circling the correct letter.

1. Which of the following words best describes Dionysius?
   - a. mercenary
   - b. tyrant
   - c. treason

2. Dionysius ordered that Damon be put to death if Pythias didn't return. What's another word for *ordered*?
   - a. decreed
   - b. defied
   - c. sought

3. What did Pythias mean when he said "robbers beset me, beating me and taking what little I had"?
   - a. Robbers tempted him to join them.
   - b. Robbers pointed him in the wrong direction.
   - c. Robbers attacked him and took his belongings.

4. The other prisoners mocked Damon, telling him that "his life would be forfeit" if Pythias didn't return. What does *forfeit* mean in this context?
   - a. saved
   - b. surrendered
   - c. very happy

5. Damon followed Pythias when Pythias was taken away by the bodyguards. Which vocabulary word best describes Damon's attitude toward the danger he was in?
   - a. sought
   - b. meager
   - c. heedless

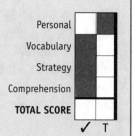

Add the numbers that you just checked to get your Personal Checklist score. Fill in your score here. Then turn to page 211 and transfer your score onto Graph 1.

Personal
Vocabulary
Strategy
Comprehension
TOTAL SCORE
✓ T

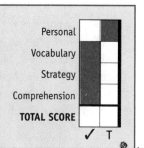

Check your answers with your teacher. Give yourself 1 point for each correct answer, and fill in your Vocabulary score here. Then turn to page 211 and transfer your score onto Graph 1.

Personal
Vocabulary
Strategy
Comprehension
TOTAL SCORE
✓ T

Strategy Check

Review the predictions you wrote for each Strategy Break. Also review the story if necessary. Then answer these questions:

1. At Strategy Break #1, if you had predicted that Dionysius would sentence Pythias to death, which clue from the story would have best supported your prediction?
   a. "The Tyrant of Syracuse had no mercy for anyone who defied him."
   b. "The tyrant made his home in Syracuse."
   c. "He locked his room at night and slept on a bed surrounded by a small moat."

2. At Strategy Break #1, which prediction would *not* have fit the story?
   a. Damon won't do anything to help Pythias.
   b. Damon will try to rescue Pythias from Dionysius.
   c. Pythias and Damon will stand up to Dionysius together.

3. At Strategy Break #2, which prediction would have been best supported by the story's clues?
   a. Pythias will not return to save Damon.
   b. Pythias will return to save Damon.
   c. Damon will escape on his own.

4. Which clue suggests that Dionysius does not believe that Pythias will return?
   a. "You doubt my power?"
   b. "There are no honest men when life or death is the prize."
   c. "I hereby sentence you to death."

5. Which clue explains why Damon trusts Pythias with his life?
   a. "Set Pythias free to settle his affairs."
   b. "Then I will die in his place."
   c. "I know him like a brother."

Comprehension Check

Review the story if necessary. Then answer these questions:

1. Why does Dionysius have one thousand bodyguards and sleep on a bed surrounded by a moat?
   a. He likes to be alone.
   b. He likes to be surrounded by his admirers.
   c. He is afraid that someone will try to kill him.

2. Why is Pythias carried away by the bodyguards of Dionysius?
   a. Pythias gives a speech in the marketplace, questioning the tyrant's right to rule.
   b. Dionysius wants to be his friend.
   c. Pythias needs to settle his affairs.

3. What deal do the two friends make with the Tyrant of Syracuse?
   a. Damon volunteers to take Pythias's place in prison and, if necessary, to die for him.
   b. Pythias volunteers to take Damon's place in prison and, if necessary, to die for him.
   c. Dionysius volunteers to take Pythias's place in prison and, if necessary, to die for him.

4. As the days went by, Dionysius visits the prison. What does he hope to see?
   a. He hopes to see Damon confident and strong.
   b. He hopes to see Damon lose faith in Pythias.
   c. He hopes to see Pythias waiting outside Damon's prison cell.

5. Why do you think Dionysius frees both men and asks them to be his friends?
   a. He is tired of his own friends.
   b. He feels sorry for Pythias because he was robbed.
   c. He is moved by their friendship and wants to know what it's like to have real friends.

Check your answers with your teacher. Give yourself 1 point for each correct answer, and fill in your Strategy score here. Then turn to page 211 and transfer your score onto Graph 1.

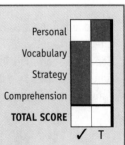

Check your answers with your teacher. Give yourself 1 point for each correct answer, and fill in your Comprehension score here. Then turn to page 211 and transfer your score onto Graph 1.

Extending

Choose one or more of these activities:

ILLUSTRATE THE LEGEND
With a partner, create an illustrated version of "Damon and Pythias." Your finished product may take whatever form you wish, from a comic book to a poster-sized collage.

WRITE A LEGEND
Write a legend about someone you know. You might write about a friend or relative. Or you might write about a famous actor, singer, or athlete. You should base your legend on the person's best or worst quality. However, the story itself doesn't have to be true. When you are finished, share the story with a friend.

EXPLORE ANCIENT GREECE
Find out more about the world in which Damon and Pythias lived. Use the resources listed on this page to learn about ancient Greece. You may want to limit yourself to a specific topic, such as family life, festivals and holidays, government, or food and drink. Share your findings in an oral or written report.

Resources

Books

Guy, J. A. *Greek Life*. Early Civilizations. Barrons Juveniles, 1998.

James, John, and Louise James. *How We Know About the Greeks*. Peter Bedrick Books, 1997.

Pearson, Anne. *Ancient Greece*. Eyewitness. DK Publishing, 2000.

Ross, Stewart. *Daily Life*. Ancient Greece. Peter Bedrick Books, 2000.

Web Site
http://members.aol.com/Donnclass/Greeklife.html
This Web site contains information about the daily life of the ancient Greeks.

Arap Sang and the Cranes

Building Background

In the selection you are about to read, Arap Sang gives a gift to the cranes. Think about the gifts you've received over the years. What are some of your favorites? What are some of your least favorites? Now think about the gifts you've given. When did you give a gift that was perfect for the receiver? When did you give a gift that didn't work out so well? Think about what makes a gift a success as you read "Arap Sang and the Cranes."

acquaintance

assistance

awkwardly

consternation

gravely

logical

pitiful

sensitive

Vocabulary Builder

1. Each word in the margin has a base word, or root word. A **root word** is a complete word by itself. However, you can add other words or word parts to a root word to make new words. For example, *work* is a root word. You can add *re-*, *-er*, and *-ing* to *work* to make *rework*, *worker*, and *working*. Identifying the root word of an unfamiliar word can sometimes help you figure out the word's meaning.

2. On the lines below, write the root word of each vocabulary word. Then use the root word to help you figure out the vocabulary word's meaning. If you have trouble with any of the words, find them in the story and use context clues. Or look them up in a dictionary.

3. Save your work. You will use it again in the Vocabulary Check.

acquaintance   root word: _____

      meaning of vocabulary word: _____

assistance   root word: _____

      meaning of vocabulary word: _____

awkwardly   root word: _____

      meaning of vocabulary word: _____

consternation   root word: _____

      meaning of vocabulary word: _____

gravely   root word: _____

            meaning of vocabulary word: _____

logical   root word: _____

            meaning of vocabulary word: _____

pitiful   root word: _____

            meaning of vocabulary word: _____

sensitive   root word: _____

            meaning of vocabulary word: _____

Strategy Builder

How to Read a Folktale

- "Arap Sang and the Cranes" is a folktale. A folktale is a simple story that has been passed from generation to generation by word of mouth. Folktales are usually told within particular families and cultures.

- Folktales tell different stories, but most have the same elements. Those elements include the following:

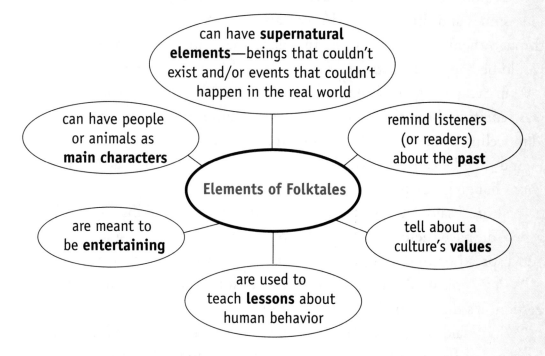

- As you read "Arap Sang and the Cranes," you will use a **concept map** to help you keep track of its folktale elements.

Arap Sang and the Cranes

By Humphrey Harman

As you read the beginning of this selection, apply the strategies that you just learned. See if you can find elements that make this story a folktale.

The people of Africa believe that before you give anything to anyone you should first carefully think out what your gift will mean to him. They are often shocked at the way white men give things, anything—tractors and trousers, guns and radios—showering them down on people's heads with no kind of thought about what they will *mean* to the people who get the presents. Like being given a camera when you can't afford to buy film. That's worse than not having a camera.

A gift is a great responsibility to the giver, they say, and after they have said that they may tell you the story of Arap Sang and the cranes. Arap Sang was a great chief and more than half a god, for in the days when he lived, great chiefs were always a little mixed up with the gods.

One day he was walking on the plain admiring the cattle. It was hot. The rains had not yet come; the ground was almost bare of grass and as hard as stone; the thorn trees gave no shade for they were just made of long spines and thin twigs and tiny leaves and the sun went straight through them. It was hot. Only the black ants didn't feel it, and they would be happy in a furnace.

Arap Sang was getting old and the sun beat down on his bald head (he was **sensitive** about this and didn't like it mentioned) and he thought: "I'm feeling things more than I used to."

And then he came across a vulture sitting in the crotch of a tree, his wings hanging down and his eyes on the lookout.

"Vulture," said Arap Sang, "I'm hot and the sun is making my head ache. You have there a fine pair of broad wings. I'd be most grateful if you'd spread them out and let an old man enjoy a patch of shade."

"Why?" croaked Vulture. He had indigestion. Vultures usually have indigestion; it's the things they eat.

"Why?" said Arap Sang mildly. "Now that's a question to which I'm not certain that I've got the answer. Why? Why, I suppose, because I ask you.

Because I'm an old man and entitled to a little **assistance** and respect. Because it wouldn't be much trouble to you. Because it's pleasant and good to help people."

"Bah!" said Vulture.

"What's that?"

"Oh, go home, Baldy, and stop bothering people; it's hot."

Arap Sang straightened himself up and his eyes flashed. He wasn't half a god for nothing, and when he was angry he could be rather a terrible old person. And he was very angry now. It was that remark about his lack of hair.

The really terrifying thing was that when he spoke he didn't shout. He spoke quietly and the words were clear and cold and hard. And all separate like hailstones.

"Vulture," he said, "you're cruel and you're selfish. I shan't forget what you've said and you won't either. NOW GET OUT!"

Arap Sang was so impressive that Vulture got up **awkwardly** and flapped off.

"Silly old fool," he said uncomfortably.

Presently he met an **acquaintance** of his (vultures don't have friends, they just have acquaintances) and they perched together on the same bough. Vulture took a close look at his companion and then another and what he saw was so funny that it cheered him up.

"He, he!" he giggled. "What's happened to you? Met with an accident? You're *bald*."

The other vulture looked sour, but at the same time you felt he might be pleased about something.

"That's good, coming from you," he said. "What have you been up to? You haven't got a feather on you above the shoulders."

Then they both felt their heads with **consternation**. It was quite true. They were bald, both of them, and so was every other vulture, the whole family, right down to this very day. Which goes to show that if you can't be ordinarily pleasant to people at least it's not wise to go insulting great chiefs who are half gods.

I said that he was rather a terrible old person.

 Stop here for the Strategy Break.

Strategy Break

If you were to create a concept map of the folktale elements in this story so far, it might look like this:

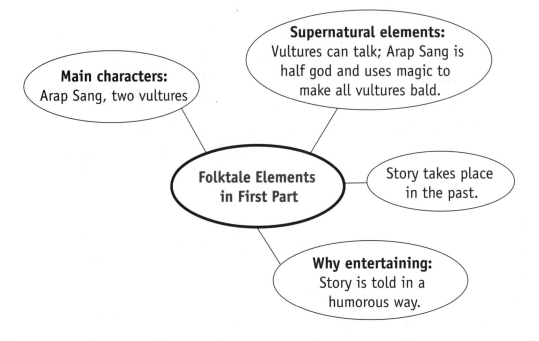

➤ **Go on reading to see what happens.**

Arap Sang walked on. He was feeling shaky. Losing his temper always upset him afterward, and doing the sort of magic that makes every vulture in the world bald in the wink of an eye takes it out of you if you aren't as young as you used to be. And he *did* want a bit of shade.

Presently he met an elephant. Elephant was panting across the plain in a tearing hurry and was most reluctant to stop when Arap Sang called to him.

"Elephant," said Arap Sang weakly. "I'm tired and I'm dizzy. I want to get to the forest and into a bit of shade but it's a long way."

"It *is* hot, isn't it?" said Elephant. "I'm off to the forest myself."

"Would you spread out your great ears and let me walk along under them?" asked Arap Sang.

"I'm sorry," said Elephant, "but you'd make my journey so slow. I must get to the forest. I've got the most terrible headache."

"Well, I've got a headache too," protested the old man.

"I'm sure," said Elephant, "and no one could be sorrier about that than I am. Is it a very big headache?"

"Shocking big," said Arap Sang.

"There now," said Elephant. "Consider how big I am compared to you and what the size of *my* headache must be."

That's elephants all over, always so **logical**. Arap Sang felt that there was something wrong with this argument but he couldn't just see where. Also he had become a little uncomfortable about all those bald vultures and he didn't want to lose his temper with anyone else. You have to be careful what you do when you're half a god. It's so dreadfully final.

"Oh, all right," he muttered.

"Knew you'd see it that way," said Elephant. "It's just what I was saying about you the other day. You can always rely on Arap Sang, I said, to behave reasonably. Well, good-by and good luck." And he hurried off in the direction of the distant forest and was soon out of sight.

Poor Arap Sang was now feeling very ill indeed. He sat on the ground, and he thought to himself: "I can't go another step unless I get some shade and if I don't get some soon I'm done for."

And there he was found by a flock of cranes. They came dancing through the white grass, stamping their long delicate legs so that the insects flew up in alarm and were at once snapped up in the cranes' beaks. They gathered round Arap Sang sitting on the ground and he looked so old and distressed that they hopped up and down with embarrassment, first on one leg then the other. "Korong! Korong!" they called softly and this happens to be their name as well.

"Good birds," whispered Arap Sang, "you must help me. If I don't reach shade soon I'll die. Help me to the forest."

"But, of course," said the cranes, and they spread their great handsome black and white wings to shade him and helped him to his feet, and together, slowly, they all crossed the plain into the trees.

Then Arap Sang sat in the shade of a fine cotton tree and felt very much better. The birds gathered round him and he looked at them and thought that he had never seen more beautiful creatures in the whole world.

"And kind. Kind as well as beautiful," he muttered. "The two don't always go together. I must reward them."

"I shan't forget your kindness," he said, "and I'll see that no one else does. Now I want each one of you to come here."

Then the cranes came one after another and bowed before him and Arap Sang stretched out his kindly old hand and gently touched each beautiful sleek head. And where he did this a golden crown appeared, and after the birds had **gravely** bowed their thanks they all flew off to the lake, their new crowns glittering in the evening sun.

Arap Sang felt quite recovered. He was very pleased with his gift to the cranes.

Two months later a crane dragged himself to the door of Arap Sang's house. It was a **pitiful** sight, thin with hunger, feathers broken and muddy from hiding in the reeds, eyes red with lack of sleep.

Arap Sang exclaimed in pity and horror.

"Great Chief," said the crane, "we beg you to take back your gift. If you don't, there'll soon be not one crane left alive for we are hunted day and night for the sake of our golden crowns."

Arap Sang listened and nodded his head in sorrow. "I'm old and I'm foolish," he said, "and I harm my friends. I had forgotten that men also were greedy and selfish and that they'll do anything for gold. Let me undo the wrong I have done by giving without thought. I'll make one more magic but that'll be the last."

Then he took their golden crowns and in their place he put a wonderful halo of feathers which they have until this day. But they still are called Crowned Cranes. ●

Strategy Follow-up

On the concept map below, list the folktale elements in the second part of this story. Begin by adding the rest of the main characters. Then add the other supernatural events. Last, fill in the rest of the concept map.

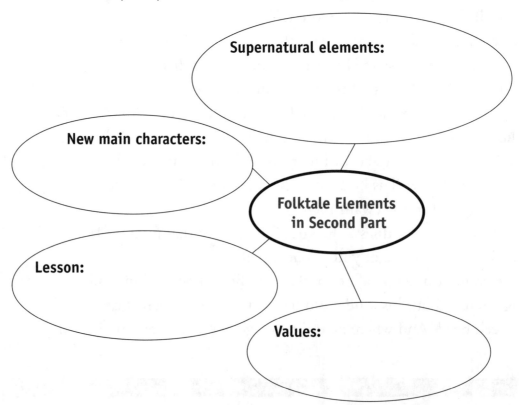

Supernatural elements:

New main characters:

Folktale Elements in Second Part

Lesson:

Values:

✓Personal Checklist

Read each question and put a check (✓) in the correct box.

1. In Building Background, how well did thinking about your own gift-giving experiences help you understand the folktale's lesson?
   - ☐ 3 (extremely well)
   - ☐ 2 (fairly well)
   - ☐ 1 (not well)

2. In the Vocabulary Builder, how many words were you able to define by using their root words and context clues?
   - ☐ 3 (6–8 words)
   - ☐ 2 (3–5 words)
   - ☐ 1 (0–2 words)

3. How well were you able to complete the concept map in the Strategy Follow-up?
   - ☐ 3 (extremely well)
   - ☐ 2 (fairly well)
   - ☐ 1 (not well)

4. How well do you understand why the cranes were hunted?
   - ☐ 3 (extremely well)
   - ☐ 2 (fairly well)
   - ☐ 1 (not well)

5. How well do you understand why Arap Sang calls himself old and foolish for giving the cranes golden crowns?
   - ☐ 3 (extremely well)
   - ☐ 2 (fairly well)
   - ☐ 1 (not well)

Vocabulary Check

Look back at the work you did in the Vocabulary Builder. Then answer each question by circling the correct letter.

1. When the vultures "felt their heads with consternation," how did they look?
   a. They looked astonished.
   b. They looked angry.
   c. They looked amused.

2. What is the root word of *sensitive*?
   a. send
   b. sent
   c. sense

3. What does the root word of *gravely* mean?
   a. burial
   b. serious
   c. rough

4. Which vocabulary word means "reasonable"?
   a. logical
   b. pitiful
   c. awkwardly

5. Which vocabulary word would you be able to figure out by using the context clue "friends"?
   a. acquaintance
   b. assistance
   c. awkwardly

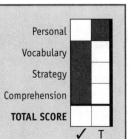

Add the numbers that you just checked to get your Personal Checklist score. Fill in your score here. Then turn to page 211 and transfer your score onto Graph 1.

Personal
Vocabulary
Strategy
Comprehension
TOTAL SCORE
✓ T

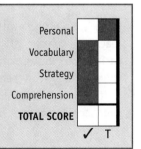

Check your answers with your teacher. Give yourself 1 point for each correct answer, and fill in your Vocabulary score here. Then turn to page 211 and transfer your score onto Graph 1.

Personal
Vocabulary
Strategy
Comprehension
TOTAL SCORE
✓ T

Strategy Check

Review the concept map that you completed in the Strategy Follow-up. Also review the rest of the story. Then answer these questions:

1. When Arap Sang touches each crane's head, a golden crown appears there. Which folktale element is this an example of?
   a. a lesson
   b. values
   c. a supernatural event

2. Which characters did you add to your concept map?
   a. Elephant, cranes
   b. Great Chief
   c. the hurt crane

3. What does the folktale tell you about traditional African values?
   a. People admired cranes.
   b. People were greedy.
   c. People respected the elderly.

4. Which of the following is a supernatural event?
   a. The cranes are hunted day and night.
   b. Arap Sang replaces the golden crowns with halos of feathers.
   c. Arap Sang sits in the shade and soon feels better.

5. What lesson about human behavior does this folktale teach?
   a. Be thoughtful and careful when you give a gift.
   b. Never walk long distances in the hot sun.
   c. Kind acts should be rewarded with expensive gifts.

Comprehension Check

Review the story if necessary. Then answer these questions:

1. According to the folktale, what is the responsibility of someone who gives a gift?
   a. to shower gifts down on someone's head
   b. to consider what the gift will mean to the receiver
   c. to return a gift if it isn't right

2. Why does Arap Sang make all vultures bald?
   a. to prevent them from being hunted
   b. because a vulture is cruel and selfish to him
   c. to make the other animals laugh

3. Elephant claims that his headache is bigger than Arap Sang's because he (Elephant) is so much bigger. What's wrong with Elephant's argument?
   a. Arap Sang is actually much bigger than Elephant.
   b. Because Arap Sang is half god, his pain is greater.
   c. Pain is not determined by the size of the sufferer.

4. Why does Arap Sang place golden crowns on the cranes' heads?
   a. because the cranes shade Arap Sang and help him to the forest
   b. because they are such beautiful creatures
   c. because they look so pitiful

5. Why was Arap Sang irresponsible when he gave the cranes golden crowns?
   a. He didn't stop to think that the crowns would be too heavy for the cranes.
   b. He forgot that greedy men would kill the cranes to get the crowns.
   c. He didn't ask the cranes whether they would prefer halos of feathers.

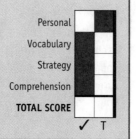

Check your answers with your teacher. Give yourself 1 point for each correct answer, and fill in your Strategy score here. Then turn to page 211 and transfer your score onto Graph 1.

Personal
Vocabulary
Strategy
Comprehension
TOTAL SCORE
✓ T

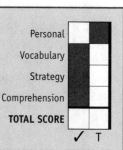

Check your answers with your teacher. Give yourself 1 point for each correct answer, and fill in your Comprehension score here. Then turn to page 211 and transfer your score onto Graph 1.

Personal
Vocabulary
Strategy
Comprehension
TOTAL SCORE
✓ T

Extending

Choose one or more of these activities:

STAGE A PERFORMANCE
With a group of classmates, perform "Arap Sang and the Cranes." Choose roles and brainstorm ideas for simple costumes. After you've had time to practice, perform your play before the class.

TELL A TALE
Folktales were originally told out loud by storytellers. Find a folktale to tell your class—or any other audience. Choose a favorite folktale or one that you find in the resources listed on this page. As you tell the tale, use gestures to act out each character's actions. Also, use different voices when you speak the characters' lines.

DRAW A CROWNED CRANE
Use your own resources or those listed on this page to find pictures of crowned cranes. Then draw a picture of one. You might draw a picture of a crane in the wild. Or you might illustrate a crane in a scene from the story.

Resources

Books
Abrahams, Roger, ed. *African American Folktales: Stories from Black Traditions in the New World.* Pantheon Fairy Tales and Folklore Library. Pantheon Books, 1999.

Bryan, Ashley. *Lion and the Ostrich Chicks.* Aladdin, 1996.

Yolen, Jane, ed. *Favorite Folktales from Around the World.* Pantheon Books, 1988.

Web Sites
http://www.darsie.net/talesofwonder/
On this Web site, you can read folktales from many parts of the world.

http://www.savingcranes.org
This Web site contains pictures and information related to cranes. Click on "Crane Species" for links to information on various types of cranes, including crowned cranes.

Elizabeth Blackwell, Pioneer Doctor

Building Background

The selection you are about to read tells about the life of Elizabeth Blackwell, who lived in the 1800s. In those days, women did not have the same opportunities that men had—particularly in the workplace. Women were not expected to work outside the home. Those who did usually worked in factories, on farms, or as servants in other people's homes. Elizabeth, however, had other ambitions. She didn't let anything stop her from achieving her goals. Think about a time when you had to struggle to get something. What obstacles did you overcome to achieve your goal?

filthy

illness

indecent

miserable

prejudiced

privately

self-doubt

unjust

Vocabulary Builder

1. Each word in the margin contains either a prefix or a suffix. A **prefix** is a word part that is added to the beginning of a word. A **suffix** is a word part that is added to the end of a word.

2. This chart defines the prefixes and suffixes contained in the vocabulary words:

Prefixes		Suffixes	
in-	not	*-able*	condition
pre-	before	*-ly*	in the manner of
self-	oneself	*-ness*	state
un-	not	*-y*	condition

3. Now write the word that each definition describes.

   a. in an independent manner _____

   b. not moral _____

   c. judged beforehand _____

   d. very dirty condition _____

e. state of being sick   _____

f. questioning yourself   _____

g. not fair   _____

h. distressed condition   _____

Strategy Builder

How to Read a Biography

- A **biography** is the story of a person's life, written by someone else. A biography is often written in time order, or **sequence**. To keep track of this sequence, writers often use **signal words,** such as *in 1837* or *when she was 24.*

- The following paragraphs are from a biography of Florence Nightingale. Notice the sequence of events as you read. Use the underlined signal words to help you.

> Florence Nightingale was born in Florence, Italy, <u>in 1820</u>. <u>When Florence was 16</u>, she claimed that she heard the voice of God. The voice told her that she had a special mission in life. Florence decided that her mission was to help others.
>
> She got her first chance <u>in 1854</u>, when the Crimean War broke out. Doctors came to respect Florence's nursing skills as she treated the wounded British soldiers.
>
> When she returned to England <u>in 1856</u>, many important officials sought her professional advice. The United States government even asked Florence's help in setting up military hospitals during the Civil War <u>(1861–1865)</u>.
>
> Florence died <u>in 1910</u>, at the age of 90.

- If you wanted to show the sequence of events in these paragraphs, you could put them on a **time line** like this one:

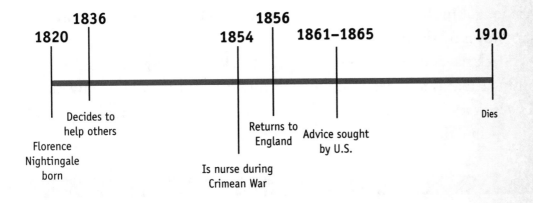

Elizabeth Blackwell, Pioneer Doctor

By Matthew G. Grant

As you read the first part of this biography, note the underlined dates and important events in Elizabeth Blackwell's life.

Finding a New Life

Little Elizabeth crouched by the upstairs window. Outside, a riot was raging. Shouting men roamed the streets of Bristol, England. Burning buildings lit up the night sky. Elizabeth was afraid.

Later, her father came home and tried to tell her why the riot had happened. "Poor people are hungry. They feel our government is unjust toward them, and they think their only hope is violence."

Samuel Blackwell was a rich sugar merchant. But he was also a deep-thinking man. He wished to help the suffering poor but he did not know how. His nine children shared his beliefs.

It was the year 1830. Before too long, the Blackwell family found out what it was like to be poor. Mr. Blackwell's business failed. He said, "We will go to America and start over again."

Elizabeth clung to the hand of her little sister, Emily, as they got on board a sailing ship. She tried to be brave as the shore of England disappeared and gray waves surged all around them.

The poorest passengers, deep in the ship's hold, took sick. Several died. Elizabeth watched with horror as the bodies were brought up, prayed over, and dropped into the sea. Her father said, "They died because they were poor. They had to travel in a dark, **filthy** hold. All over the world, people die needlessly because they are poor. Somehow, we must find a way to help them."

Eleven-year-old Elizabeth nodded.

Mr. Blackwell started a new sugar business in New York. But his conscience got in the way of his making a living. This happened because sugar was grown by slaves.

"Black slaves deserve to be free!" said Blackwell. "How can I carry on a business that is founded upon human misery?" But it was the only business he knew. Once more he failed to prosper. In 1837 he took the family to Cincinnati, Ohio. Not long after, Samuel Blackwell died.

A Woman's Work

Elizabeth Blackwell, aged 16, had to go to work. Unlike most well-to-do young women of the time, she had been well educated. So she became a teacher in Kentucky. Despite her youth, she was forceful and determined to succeed.

Elizabeth was impatient when men talked about how "inferior" women were. She, like many other women of that time, was becoming aware of women's rights.

Was not one of those rights the right to earn a good living? Even the best woman teacher earned far less than a man. Wasn't her mind as good as that of any man she knew? Of course it was! If only men would give women a chance to prove themselves!

The years went by. She felt she was wasting her life. Then, <u>when she was 24</u>, she happened to visit a friend named Mary who was dying.

Mary took Elizabeth's hand. "The worst of my **illness** is being treated by a gruff, unfeeling doctor. If only there were women doctors!"

Elizabeth agreed. And then her friend said, "You are young and strong. You could become a doctor."

 Stop here for the Strategy Break.

Strategy Break

If you were to show the most important events in Elizabeth Blackwell's life so far, your time line might look like the following. Notice that Elizabeth's birthdate has been supplied.

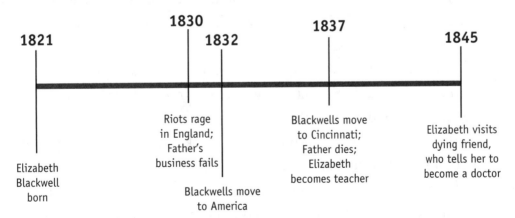

As you continue reading, keep paying attention to the events in Elizabeth's life. Also keep looking for signal words. At the end of this selection, you will create a time line of your own.

Go on reading.

Opening Doors

It was impossible! Women did not become doctors. But Elizabeth could not forget her dying friend's words. For weeks she thought about it. Then she announced to her family, "I am going to try to become a doctor." Elizabeth had great difficulty finding a place to study. No medical school would admit a woman. So she studied **privately** at first, helped by Quaker doctors who believed in women's rights.

In 1847 she applied to Geneva Medical College, a small school in New York. Largely as a joke, the school admitted her. The teachers and students waited for her to make a fool of herself and quit.

In those days, "nice" women fainted at the sight of blood. They never talked about the workings of the body. But Elizabeth was not silly. She felt she could learn anything a man could learn—and she proved it. Students who had laughed at her began to respect her courage and her fine mind. The jokes stopped—but the townspeople of Geneva were sure she was some kind of **indecent** woman. No one in town would speak to her.

During her summer vacation, she helped treat the sick at Philadelphia's huge Blockley Almshouse. The most **miserable** of the sick poor came to this place. Elizabeth found out how truly ignorant she was as she tried to help them. "I must learn more!" she said. "There is so much work do be done among the sick. Somehow, I must get other women to help me!"

That fall, she returned to school. At that time, a medical degree required only a short period of study. Elizabeth Blackwell became a doctor of medicine on January 23, 1849. She was the first woman physician to graduate in the United States.

She went to Paris to learn more about the diseases of women and children. While treating a sick baby, she was infected with an eye disease. It caused her to lose the sight of one eye.

She needed a lot of courage in the weeks that followed. She suffered pain and **self-doubt** as well.

She went to England and became a friend of the famous nurse, Florence Nightingale. In 1850 she received good news. Lydia Folger had become the first American-born woman doctor—and other women were seeking medical degrees. Even Emily, Elizabeth's younger sister, wanted to become a doctor.

Founder of a Hospital

Dr. Elizabeth Blackwell returned to New York in 1851. Her great desire was to help the sick poor. But at first, she was not able to practice medicine. People were still very **prejudiced** against a woman doctor.

Little by little, women patients came to her. She became used to their saying, "Why, you are a proper doctor after all!"

In 1853 she opened a dispensary, a kind of clinic, for treating poor women and children. She was joined in this work by her sister Emily, who graduated from medical school the following year. The two women begged their wealthy friends to help them start a real hospital.

Elizabeth and Emily Blackwell's dream came true in 1857, when the New York Infirmary for Women and Children opened its doors. It was the first true hospital for women, run by women doctors, anywhere in the world.

Not only did the hospital treat the poor, but it also trained nurses. A black woman doctor, Rebecca Cole, joined the staff and set up the first "visiting doctor" service ever known in a large American city.

In 1868, the Infirmary opened its own medical college for women. Then Elizabeth received a letter from England, begging her to come there and "do for the women of England what you have done in America." She left the Infirmary in the capable hands of Emily and returned to the land of her birth in 1869. There she lived and worked for another 40 years, a champion of women's rights. She died May 31, 1910. ●

Strategy Follow-up

Work on this activity with a partner or group of classmates. On a long piece of paper, copy the time line from the Strategy Break. Then add the following time line. Fill in the dates and information for 1847–1910. Some of the information has been filled in for you.

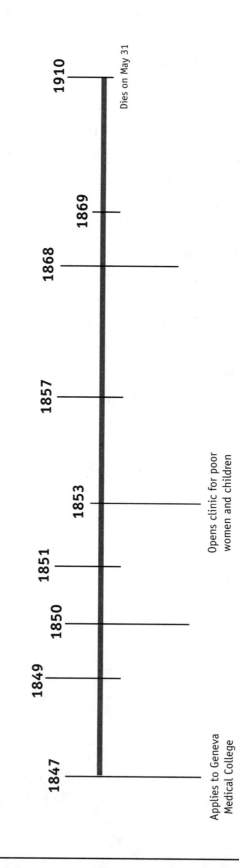

1847 — Applies to Geneva Medical College

1849

1850

1851

1853 — Opens clinic for poor women and children

1857

1868

1869

1910 — Dies on May 31

✓Personal Checklist

Read each question and put a check (✓) in the correct box.

1. In Building Background, how well did thinking about the obstacles you've overcome help you understand what Elizabeth Blackwell faced in her life?
   - ☐ 3 (extremely well)
   - ☐ 2 (fairly well)
   - ☐ 1 (not well)

2. In the Vocabulary Builder, how well were you able to use a word's prefix or suffix to help you figure out its meaning?
   - ☐ 3 (extremely well)
   - ☐ 2 (fairly well)
   - ☐ 1 (not well)

3. In the Strategy Follow-up, how well were you able to record the events in Elizabeth's life?
   - ☐ 3 (extremely well)
   - ☐ 2 (fairly well)
   - ☐ 1 (not well)

4. How well do you understand why Elizabeth decided to become a doctor?
   - ☐ 3 (extremely well)
   - ☐ 2 (fairly well)
   - ☐ 1 (not well)

5. How well do you understand the importance of Elizabeth's achievements to other women?
   - ☐ 3 (extremely well)
   - ☐ 2 (fairly well)
   - ☐ 1 (not well)

Vocabulary Check

Look back at the work you did in the Vocabulary Builder. Then answer each question by circling the correct letter.

1. Which vocabulary word means "questioning yourself"?
   - a. self-doubt
   - b. indecent
   - c. miserable

2. Which of these prefixes does *not* mean "not"?
   - a. un-
   - b. in-
   - c. pre-

3. Which vocabulary word means "judged beforehand"?
   - a. filthy
   - b. prejudiced
   - c. privately

4. Elizabeth Blackwell studied medicine privately at first. What does *privately* mean?
   - a. very dirty condition
   - b. in an independent manner
   - c. distressed condition

5. What is the opposite of *indecent*?
   - a. just
   - b. not moral
   - c. moral

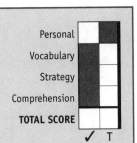

Add the numbers that you just checked to get your Personal Checklist score. Fill in your score here. Then turn to page 211 and transfer your score onto Graph 1.

Personal
Vocabulary
Strategy
Comprehension
TOTAL SCORE
✓ T

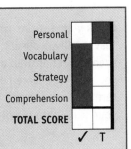

Check your answers with your teacher. Give yourself 1 point for each correct answer, and fill in your Vocabulary score here. Then turn to page 211 and transfer your score onto Graph 1.

Personal
Vocabulary
Strategy
Comprehension
TOTAL SCORE
✓ T

Strategy Check

Review the time line you completed in the Strategy Follow-up. Then answer these questions:

1. What event followed the failure of Mr. Blackwell's business?

    a. Riots raged in England.

    b. The family moved to Cincinnati.

    c. The family moved to America.

2. What happened when Elizabeth was 24?

    a. A dying friend urged Elizabeth to become a doctor.

    b. Elizabeth died on May 31.

    c. Her father died.

3. Which of these three events happened first?

    a. Elizabeth applied to Geneva Medical College.

    b. Elizabeth opened a clinic for poor women and children.

    c. Elizabeth returned to England.

4. What happened in 1849?

    a. A friend told Elizabeth that she should become a doctor.

    b. Lydia Folger became the first American-born woman doctor.

    c. Elizabeth became the first woman doctor of medicine in the United States.

5. What happened one year before Elizabeth returned to England?

    a. She opened the New York Infirmary for Women and Children.

    b. She opened a clinic for poor women and children.

    c. Her infirmary opened its own medical college for women.

Comprehension Check

Review the selection if necessary. Then answer these questions:

1. Which sentence *best* describes Elizabeth Blackwell's father?

    a. He was a deep-thinking man who wished to help the poor.

    b. He was a rich sugar merchant.

    c. He carried on a business founded on human misery.

2. What made Elizabeth impatient?

    a. having to earn her own living

    b. having to work as a teacher

    c. hearing men talk about how "inferior" women were

3. Why did the Geneva Medical College admit Elizabeth?

    a. because the teachers and students believed in women's rights

    b. because the teachers and students wanted to see her make a fool of herself

    c. because the teachers and students respected Elizabeth's courage and fine mind

4. What happened to Elizabeth when she went to Paris?

    a. No one would speak to her.

    b. She realized how truly ignorant she was.

    c. She was infected with an eye disease.

5. Why did Elizabeth return to England?

    a. She received a letter begging her to come there and "do for the women of England what you have done in America."

    b. She wanted to set up the first "visiting doctor" service ever known.

    c. She and her sister went to beg their wealthy friends to help them start a real hospital.

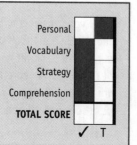

Check your answers with your teacher. Give yourself 1 point for each correct answer, and fill in your Strategy score here. Then turn to page 211 and transfer your score onto Graph 1.

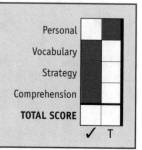

Check your answers with your teacher. Give yourself 1 point for each correct answer, and fill in your Comprehension score here. Then turn to page 211 and transfer your score onto Graph 1.

Extending

Choose one or more of these activities:

SUMMARIZE THE SELECTION

Use your time line to summarize what happened in "Elizabeth Blackwell, Pioneer Doctor." Include signal words to clarify the order of events. Share your summary with a partner. Can he or she follow the order of events?

MAKE A TIME LINE

Think about the most important events from your own life. Then make a time line that presents the most significant dates and events. Illustrate your time line with photographs and drawings if you wish.

LEARN ABOUT OTHER WOMEN DOCTORS

Elizabeth Blackwell paved the way for women in medicine. Consult one of the resources listed on this page to find out more about other women who became doctors. Present your findings in an oral or written report.

Resources

Books

Baker, Rachel. *The First Woman Doctor: The Story of Elizabeth Blackwell, M.D.* Bt Bound, 1999.

Garza, Hedda, and Robert Green. *Women in Medicine.* Women Then—Women Now. Franklin Watts, 1994.

Henry, Joanne Landers. *Elizabeth Blackwell: Girl Doctor.* Childhood of Famous Americans. Aladdin, 1996.

Latham, Jean Lee. *Elizabeth Blackwell: Pioneer Woman Doctor.* Discover Biographies. Chelsea House, 1991.

Stille, Darlene R. *Extraordinary Women of Medicine.* Extraordinary People. Children's Book Press, 1997.

Web Sites

http://www.greatwomen.org/women.php?action
=viewone&id=20
This Web site contains a brief biography and a photo of Elizabeth Blackwell.

http://www.nlm.nih.gov/hmd/blackwell/
This online exhibit tells about the life and career of Elizabeth Blackwell.

LESSON 14 Jump for Center

accurate

arduously

congratulated

disconsolately

flubbed

petulantly

pivoted

retorted

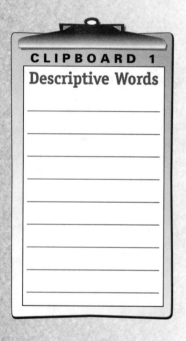

CLIPBOARD 1
Descriptive Words

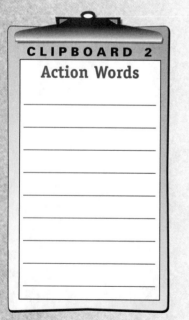

CLIPBOARD 2
Action Words

Building Background

In the selection you are about to read, the main character, Pete Langdon, wants to improve his skill as a basketball player. What have you done to improve your ability in something that's important to you? Maybe you improved your performance in a school subject by increasing your homework and study time. Or maybe you've worked to improve your ability on the tennis court by practicing your backhand. Think about the steps you've taken to improve something in your life. Then get together with a partner to exchange your secrets for success.

Vocabulary Builder

1. Study the vocabulary words in the margin. Each word is either a descriptive word or an action word. A **descriptive** word describes how someone or something looks or acts. An **action** word tells what someone did. List the descriptive words on Clipboard #1. List the action words on Clipboard #2.

2. Then read the following sentences. Underline the context clues that help you understand the boldfaced vocabulary words.

   a. Coach said that Josh really messed up when he **flubbed** the throw.

   b. We cried **disconsolately** when we heard the sad news.

   c. Her numbers weren't incorrect; in fact, they were **accurate**.

   d. When I asked Jan a question, she **retorted**, "No way."

   e. Alicia grabbed the ball **petulantly**, but her anger was short-lived.

   f. He **pivoted**, but halfway into the turn, he slipped and fell down.

   g. He worked **arduously**, or very hard, to learn the dance step.

   h. The other team **congratulated** us with "high fives" after we won the game.

3. Save your work. You will use it again in the Vocabulary Check.

Strategy Builder

Identifying Problems and Solutions in Stories

- In Lesson 8 you learned that the plot in most stories revolves around a **problem** that the main character or characters try to solve. Sometimes they try more than one **solution**. By the end, they usually come up with the solution that works—the **end result**.

- As you read the following paragraph, notice Maya's problem and how she tries to solve it.

> Maya knew that she was the best soccer player in seventh grade, but convincing Coach Sanchez of that was going to be tough. The coach didn't think girls should be on his team. Maya went to the first day of tryouts, but somehow Coach Sanchez never got around to calling on her to play. So, on the second and last day of tryouts, Maya tried something different. She stuffed her hair under a baseball cap and signed up for tryouts as Mike. When the coach called "Mike" up, Maya dazzled everyone with her dribbling and passes. After she was through, Maya took off the cap. She told the surprised coach that she just wanted a chance. "Well," said Coach Sanchez, "now you've got it. You're on the team."

- If you wanted to show the problem and solutions in the paragraph above, you could put them on a problem-solution frame. It would look something like this:

What is the problem?
Maya wants to be on the soccer team.

Why is it a problem?
Coach Sanchez doesn't want girls on his team.

Solutions	**Results**
1. Maya goes to the first day of tryouts.	1. The coach doesn't call her up to play.
2. Maya tries out as "Mike" and dazzles everyone with her ability.	2. **END RESULT:** Coach Sanchez puts Maya on the team.

Jump for Center

By Barbara O. Webb

As you read the first part of this story, notice Pete Langdon's problem. (It is circled.) Then notice the solutions he tries and their results. (His solutions are underlined once. The results are underlined twice.) Why does Pete keep trying new solutions?

Pete Langdon and a neighbor, Margaret Silver Moon, were practicing basketball shots in the alley behind Pete's apartment building. Pete's father had put up a basketball hoop and backboard over the garage door, and Pete and his friends spent endless hours practicing free throws, lay-ups, and jump shots. Margaret was on their school's junior-high team for the second year. She was a good player.

This year Pete had tried out for the team sponsored by the Teen Sports Association. He was hoping to play center on the team because he was one of the tallest boys at school. He felt that being tall gave him an excellent chance to be chosen. But he had a tremendous problem with jumping high enough to make good lay-up shots, and he **flubbed** jump shots miserably.

Pete remembered the basketball tryouts last Saturday with embarrassment. He had gone into the gym with a lot of confidence. He was definitely the tallest player there. He even noticed the coach looking at him and smiling.

Pete impatiently waited to get through the warm-up exercises so he could begin to show his stuff. During passing practice he dribbled and passed with assurance.

"Nice passing there, Pete," the coach said as Pete directed crisp, **accurate** passes to his teammates. "Now let's try some jump balls."

Pete tensed his body as he stood facing Charlie Mack at center. Charlie was a good two inches shorter than Pete, but when the coach tossed up the ball, Charlie leaped up and whacked it before Pete even got off the floor. The coach frowned. "Let's try that again," he said.

At the end of the tryouts the coach drew Pete aside to give him some pointers on jumping. "Practice some more, Pete," said the coach, "and we'll see how you do during scrimmage." Pete could see the coach was disappointed.

This week Pete had been making a valiant effort to follow the coach's instructions. He even jumped rope as boxers do when they work to get springiness in their feet. But still it did no good. Margaret could out-jump him every time they practiced—and she was four inches shorter than he was.

"It's my legs," Pete complained to Margaret. "They're lead weights."

"You need to get some real spring in your jumps," said a voice from behind them. "If you could get more lift, you'd be one of the best players in the neighborhood." It was Larry Córdoba, who lived across the alley from Pete.

Pete **retorted** with a sneer. "What would you know about it? Anybody who takes ballet can't know much about basketball."

"Aw, Pete, quit teasing Larry about taking ballet," Margaret said in a reasonable manner. "People should be able to do the things they like. Larry just enjoys dancing better than sports."

"That's all right," said Larry sarcastically. "I can see why this fellow is uneasy about making center on the Association team. He can't even jump three inches off the ground."

In a flash Larry raced over and took the ball from Pete's hands. The dancer **pivoted**, dribbled toward the basket, and made an effortless lay-up shot, putting the ball easily through the hoop. Larry wasn't tall, but he certainly moved swiftly and leaped like an impala.

Pete grabbed up the bouncing ball **petulantly** and turned to go home. He knew he had a problem with jumping, but he didn't need any ballet dancer to tell him so and show him up.

 Stop here for the Strategy Break.

Strategy Break

If you were to create a problem-solution frame for the story so far, it might look like this:

What is the problem?
Pete has a tremendous problem with jumping high enough to make good lay-up shots, and he flubbed jump shots miserably.

Why is it a problem?
He hopes to play center but won't be chosen unless he can jump.

Solutions	Results
1. Pete follows the coach's instructions.	1. It does no good.
2. He jumps rope to get springiness in his feet.	2. His legs are still like lead weights.

As you continue reading, keep paying attention to what Pete does to try to solve his problem. Underline each solution once and each result twice. At the end of the story, you will create a problem-solution frame of your own.

 Go on reading to see what happens.

Pete worked **arduously** for three weeks, but at the first practice game the coach picked Charlie Mack for center. Pete flopped down on the bench **disconsolately**. He thought, "Larry was right about me. I'd do *anything* to learn how to jump right. Anything?"

That afternoon Pete's heart was pounding as he knocked on Larry's door. He swallowed hard when Larry peered out.

"Hi . . . I . . . uh . . . look, I'm sorry I teased you about taking ballet. Can you really show me something to help me jump better?" he blurted out.

Larry blinked. Then he stepped back. "Sure. Come on in."

In the living room Larry had Pete take off his shoes. Larry explained how to use the legs and feet as springs. He told Pete to start from bent knees with heels on the floor. Then he should pull up with the thighs, and push off from the feet—first from the heels, then from the balls of the feet, and then the final important push off from the toes.

Larry showed Pete exercises to develop strong, springy feet. When Pete was ready to leave after forty-five minutes, Larry said, "They're powerful exercises, Pete. If you do them regularly and carefully, you'll notice a difference."

Pete felt better than he had for a long time. He had been amazed to learn from Larry that sometimes coaches recommend ballet for their players. He thought about the pivot baseball players have to make, about the running and jumping of track stars. Crazy, but maybe there was some connection between ballet and sports.

In a few weeks Pete's team was playing the Clinton Park Reds. Margaret and Larry came to watch the game and cheer Pete on. But Charlie Mack started at center. Pete sat on the bench. By the end of the third quarter of the game, the score was 29–27 in favor of the Reds. Charlie Mack was exhausted and puffing hard. The coach signaled to Pete. Pete leaped up from the bench.

On the first jump ball, Pete felt himself rise high in the air and heard the solid whack of his palm against the ball. Out of the corner of his eye, he saw a grin of appreciation on the coach's face.

Back and forth the ball went, with first one team scoring, then the other. The crowd roared with excitement. Then, with just a half-minute to play, the score was tied, 35–35. The Reds had the ball. Their forward drove in for a lay-up shot. A miss! Four players jumped for the rebound. Pete, leaping like a kangaroo, outjumped them all to capture the ball.

With a beautiful long pass Pete zoomed the ball down the court. One of his teammates caught it, pivoted free, and made an easy basket for the win, 37–35. The crowd shrieked its approval. Larry and Margaret bounded down from the stands and **congratulated** Pete.

The coach came up to the three friends and patted Pete on the shoulder. "You really pulled it out with that rebound jump," he said. "I thought your feet were springs."

Pete grinned at Larry. "Thanks," he said. ●

Strategy Follow-up

Now create a problem-solution frame for the second part of "Jump for Center." For the problem box, use the information from the Strategy Break. Fill in the solution box with information from the second part of the story. Don't forget to label the end result.

What is the problem?
Pete has a tremendous problem with jumping high enough to make good lay-up shots, and he flubbed jump shots miserably.

Why is it a problem?
He hopes to play center but won't be chosen unless he can jump.

Solutions	Results

✓Personal Checklist

Read each question and put a check (✓) in the correct box.

1. How well did your discussion in Building Background help you understand Pete Langdon's efforts to improve his jumping?
   - ☐ 3 (extremely well)
   - ☐ 2 (fairly well)
   - ☐ 1 (not well)

2. In the Vocabulary Builder, how many words were you able to identify as either descriptive or action words?
   - ☐ 3 (6–8 words)
   - ☐ 2 (3–5 words)
   - ☐ 1 (0–2 words)

3. How well were you able to complete the problem-solution frame in the Strategy Follow-up?
   - ☐ 3 (extremely well)
   - ☐ 2 (fairly well)
   - ☐ 1 (not well)

4. How well do you understand why Pete asked Larry for help?
   - ☐ 3 (extremely well)
   - ☐ 2 (fairly well)
   - ☐ 1 (not well)

5. How well do you understand why a ballet dancer was able to help a basketball player?
   - ☐ 3 (extremely well)
   - ☐ 2 (fairly well)
   - ☐ 1 (not well)

Vocabulary Check

Look back at the work you did in the Vocabulary Builder. Then answer each question by circling the correct letter.

1. Which of the following is *not* an action word?
   - a. pivoted
   - b. petulantly
   - c. retorted

2. Which of the following is *not* a description word?
   - a. congratulated
   - b. accurate
   - c. disconsolately

3. What context clue helped you figure out what *flubbed* means?
   - a. the throw
   - b. really
   - c. messed up

4. What context clue helped you figure out what *arduously* means?
   - a. very hard
   - b. the dance step
   - c. learn

5. Pete sits down on the bench disconsolately after the coach picks Charlie Mack to be center. What does *disconsolately* mean?
   - a. very happy
   - b. very sad
   - c. very angry

Add the numbers that you just checked to get your Personal Checklist score. Fill in your score here. Then turn to page 211 and transfer your score onto Graph 1.

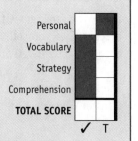

Check your answers with your teacher. Give yourself 1 point for each correct answer, and fill in your Vocabulary score here. Then turn to page 211 and transfer your score onto Graph 1.

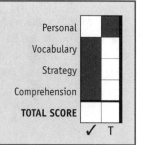

Strategy Check

Review the problem-solution frame you completed in the Strategy Follow-up. Also review the selection if necessary. Then answer these questions:

1. What solution does Pete try after he tries jumping rope?
   a. He attaches springs to his legs.
   b. He tells Larry that a dancer can't help him.
   c. He asks Larry to show him how to jump better.

2. What is the result of this solution?
   a. Larry shows Pete ballet exercises to help him develop strong, springy feet.
   b. Pete asks Margaret for help.
   c. The springs help Pete jump higher.

3. What helps Pete build up his legs?
   a. jumping rope
   b. doing the exercises that Larry shows him
   c. practicing jump shots

4. How does Pete feel after he builds up his legs?
   a. no different than before
   b. better than he has for a long time
   c. petulant

5. What is the end result?
   a. Pete jumps, captures the ball, and passes it to a teammate, who makes the game-winning basket.
   b. Pete makes the game-winning basket.
   c. The coach pats Pete on the shoulder.

Comprehension Check

Review the story if necessary. Then answer these questions:

1. Why does Pete think he has an excellent chance to play center on the Teen Sports Association basketball team?
   a. He has played for two years on his school's junior-high team.
   b. He can make good lay-up shots.
   c. He is one of the tallest boys at school.

2. Why is the coach disappointed with Pete after basketball tryouts?
   a. Pete didn't try hard.
   b. Pete can't jump very well.
   c. Pete's passing and dribbling skills were weak.

3. Why doesn't Pete think that Larry can help him?
   a. Pete doesn't think that a ballet dancer knows anything about basketball.
   b. Larry is too busy.
   c. Larry can't jump very high.

4. How do you think Larry feels when Pete asks him for help?
   a. Larry probably feels embarrassed.
   b. Larry probably feels surprised.
   c. Larry probably feels angry.

5. Who does Pete thank after his team beats the Clinton Park Reds?
   a. He thanks his coach.
   b. He thanks Charlie Mack.
   c. He thanks Larry.

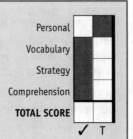

Check your answers with your teacher. Give yourself 1 point for each correct answer, and fill in your Strategy score here. Then turn to page 211 and transfer your score onto Graph 1.

Personal
Vocabulary
Strategy
Comprehension
TOTAL SCORE
✓ T

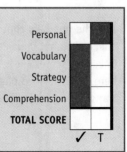

Check your answers with your teacher. Give yourself 1 point for each correct answer, and fill in your Comprehension score here. Then turn to page 211 and transfer your score onto Graph 1.

Personal
Vocabulary
Strategy
Comprehension
TOTAL SCORE
✓ T

Extending

Choose one or both of these activities:

SOLVE A PROBLEM IN YOUR SCHOOL

With a partner, identify a problem in your school and find out what has been done to solve it. Then create a problem-solution frame to describe the problem, the solution or solutions that have been tried, and their results. If the problem has not yet been solved, add some solutions of your own to the chart, along with the end result you expect.

REPORT ON BASKETBALL OR BALLET

Choose one or more of the resources listed on this page and find out more about either basketball or ballet. For example, if you want to learn about basketball, you might find out about past or present players, the history of the sport, or the progress of a local team. If you want to learn about ballet, you might find out how dancers train or what they have in common with basketball players and other athletes. Share your findings in an oral or written report.

Resources

Books

Castle, Kate. *Ballet.* Houghton Mifflin, 2002.

Jensen, Julie, Jim Klinzing, and Mike Klinzing. *Beginning Basketball.* Beginning Sports. Lerner, 1996.

Klinzing, James E., and Mike Klinzing. *Fundamental Basketball.* Fundamental Sports. Lerner, 1996.

Leggat, Bonnie-Alise. *Punt, Pass, and Point.* Landmark, 1992.

Sullivan, George. *All About Basketball.* Bt Bound, 2000.

Vancil, Mark. *NBA Basketball Basics.* Sterling, 1995.

Web Sites

http://www.fwdballet.com/kids/index.asp?ID=0101
This "Kids" page of the Texas Ballet Theater Web site includes information about ballet history and terms.

http://www.ncaa.org/sports/basketball/
This "Basketball" page of the National Collegiate Athletic Association Web site presents rules and other information related to men's and women's college basketball.

In the Tiger's Lair

Building Background

In the selection you are about to read, you will learn about tigers. Of course, you probably already know something about these "big cats." You may have seen them at the zoo or on television. Or you may have heard or read about them. Think about what you've learned or heard about tigers. Then get together with a partner and write down what you know. For example, you might explain where tigers live or what they look like. You might also draw a picture of a tiger.

camouflage

carcass

gestation

lair

pant

prey

pug marks

stalking

Vocabulary Builder

1. In Lesson 3 you learned that **specialized vocabulary words** all relate to a particular topic. For example, in "How Buildings Take Shape," the specialized words *applications, architect, collapse, horizontal, rigid, truss,* and *vertical* all relate to the construction of buildings.

2. Draw a line from each specialized vocabulary word in Column 1 to its definition in Column 2. Then think about how each word might be used in an article about tigers.

COLUMN 1	COLUMN 2
camouflage	animal hunted for food
carcass	wild animal's home
gestation	to hide using protective coloring
lair	quietly hunting
pant	animal's dead body
prey	pawprints
pug marks	breathe heavily
stalking	period of pregnancy

3. Save your work. You will use it again in the Vocabulary Check.

Strategy Builder

How to Read an Informational Article

- You have learned that an **informational article** gives facts and details about a topic. You also have learned that an informational article is organized into **main ideas** and **supporting details**.

- Main ideas are often stated in sentences that come at or near the beginning of a paragraph or section. A **main idea sentence** sums up what a paragraph or section is about. The rest of the paragraph or section contains details that support, or tell more about, the main idea.

- The following paragraph is from an informational article on cats. The main idea sentence is underlined once. Details that support the main idea are underlined twice.

Your Pet: Cat or Small Tiger?

<u>Cats have a lot in common with tigers</u>. For one thing, both animals are <u>fierce hunters</u>, who silently hunt down their victims before pouncing on them. Cats and tigers are also <u>great sleepers</u>, catnapping up to 18 hours a day. In addition, both types of cat share some charming qualities: they are both <u>very playful</u> and they both <u>purr when content</u>.

- If you wanted to show the main idea sentence and supporting details on a graphic organizer, you could put them on a **main idea table**. It would look like this:

Your Pet: Cat or Small Tiger?

Main Idea Sentence: Cats have a lot in common with tigers.			
Detail #1 fierce hunters	**Detail #2** great sleepers	**Detail #3** very playful	**Detail #4** purr when content

In the Tiger's Lair

By Don Arthur Torgersen

As you read the beginning of this informational article, you can apply some of the strategies that you just learned. The main idea sentence in the section on a tiger's size is underlined once. Supporting details are underlined twice.

On a moonlit winter night, a large tiger walks quietly through the snow in a Siberian forest. When he reaches open meadow, he begins to run, gliding across the snow in long bounds. With one great leap of nearly twenty feet, he plunges into a huge snowdrift and begins to roll around in the snow like a kitten.

In India, on a warm day, thousands of miles to the south of Siberia, a village woman cuts tall yellow grass with a sickle. Suddenly, she hears a deep growl. She drops her sickle, freezes, and screams *"Bagh! Bagh!"* "Tiger! Tiger!" A tigress, who was resting in its **lair**, rises out of the grass and swings one paw halfheartedly at the woman. Then the tigress turns and runs off into the bamboo forest, leaving heavy **pug marks** in the mud.

It is a hot, humid day on an Indonesian island. The lush jungle growth is dripping with water. A few miles offshore, a man sits in a small wooden boat, fishing. He is surprised to see a tiger swimming near his boat. He begins to row away as fast as he can because he had once heard a story about a tiger that snatched a fisherman right out of a boat. But this tiger was only swimming to shore from another island.

Siberia, India, and Indonesia are three distant places where tigers live. They also live in China, Korea, and other parts of Asia that have a variety of climates and habitats. Tigers live in cold northern forests, hot southern jungles, swampland, grassland, bamboo forest, and along river valleys.

Tigers are the largest of all cats. They are very closely related to lions, even though their color, markings, and outward appearances are different.

The word *tiger* comes from the ancient Persian-Greek word *tigris*, which meant "arrow." The Persians thought that the tiger moved swiftly, like an arrow.

A large male tiger is about ten feet long from the tip of his nose to the tip of his tail. He weighs about 450 pounds. A large female is about eight feet long and weighs about 350 pounds. Both male and female tigers stand about three and one-half feet tall at the shoulders.

A few Bengal and Siberian tigers stand four feet tall at the shoulders and weigh 550 to 600 pounds. The Siberian tiger tends to be heavier than India's famous Bengal tiger and has thicker fur. An occasional rare tiger weighs 700 pounds or more.

 Stop here for the Strategy Break.

Strategy Break

If you were to create a main idea table for the paragraphs that tell about a tiger's size, it might look like this:

In the Tiger's Lair

Main Idea Sentence: Tigers are the largest of all cats.

Detail #1	Detail #2	Detail #3	Detail #4	Detail #5
A large male tiger is about ten feet long and weighs about 450 pounds.	A large female is about eight feet long and weighs about 350 pounds.	Male and female tigers stand about three and one-half feet tall.	A few Bengal and Siberian tigers stand four feet tall and weigh 550 to 600 pounds.	A rare tiger weighs 700 pounds or more.

As you continue reading, keep looking for main ideas and supporting details. At the end of this article, you will use some of them to create a main idea table of your own.

Go on reading.

Tiger coats are yellowish or reddish-orange with dark stripes and various white markings. The tiger's stripes help **camouflage** the animal when it is **stalking** in tall grass or forest shadows. Tigers of the southern jungles tend to be more brightly colored than those of the northern forests.

No two tigers have the same markings. Even the markings on one side of a tiger's body are different from those on the other side.

In Asia there is a saying: "A tiger wanders two thousand miles to find its **prey** but always returns to its lair." Actually, a tiger often has several lairs. Each is located in a different part of its hunting territory. One lair might be in a rocky crevice near a waterfall. Another lair might be beneath some fallen trees several hundred miles away. Still another might be in a bamboo thicket near the edge of a river. Shade and water are important to tigers. They dislike heat and often **pant** heavily to keep cool.

The tiger hunts alone, wandering over a vast territory to find prey. A hunting range of one thousand to two thousand square miles is not uncommon for a tiger.

Various species of deer are the favorite prey of many tigers. In Siberia, tigers also prey on elk, wild boar, bears, wolves, and lynxes. In India, tigers prey on sambar deer, chital deer, black buck, large nilgai antelope, wild pigs, buffalo, and even langur monkeys. Tigers snatch salmon and other fish right out of streams, and even eat red jungle fowl and peacocks. Tigers occasionally raid domestic cattle herds.

A tiger works very hard for its food. When stalking deer, twenty attempts may be made before one is successful. In most stalks, the prey animal is sprung on from behind, grabbed with fangs and claws, bowled over, and killed with a suffocating bite to its throat. After the kill, the tiger roars loudly. Then it tries to drag the **carcass** near shade and water. There it takes two or three days to eat the kill, depending on the size of the animal. The tiger sleeps between feedings.

Tigers have been known to share their kill with other tigers or tigresses and their cubs.

Sometimes, tigers eat grass, as do many cats. It is doubtful if the grass provides nutrition, but the roughage might aid the tiger's digestion.

Female tigers bear young every three or four years. **Gestation** lasts 95 to 112 days. Tiger cubs are playful creatures, who cuff each other with fat little paws, roll and wrestle, nip and snarl, and chase insects. They stay with their mother for two to three years before they go off on their own.

Tigers have few natural enemies, except for wild dogs that attack in packs. But human beings have been very harsh on tigers. In 1930, there were about 40 thousand tigers in India. But, during World War II, crowds of people followed tigers to their lairs and shot them from jeeps. Others were killed by poisoned meats, poachers who wanted to sell tiger pelts to fashion designers, and poison chemicals used in insecticides. Today, there are fewer than two thousand tigers living in India. Their numbers are also dwindling in other parts of Asia. ●

Strategy Follow-up

Now create a main idea table of your own. Some of the table has been filled in for you.

In the Tiger's Lair

Main Idea Sentence: Human beings have been very harsh on tigers.

Detail #1	**Detail #2**	**Detail #3**	**Detail #4**
In 1930,	During World War II,	Others were killed	Today,

✓Personal Checklist

Read each question and put a check (✓) in the correct box.

1. How well did you understand the information presented in this article?
   - ☐ 3 (extremely well)
   - ☐ 2 (fairly well)
   - ☐ 1 (not well)

2. In Building Background, how well were you able to write what you already know about tigers?
   - ☐ 3 (extremely well)
   - ☐ 2 (fairly well)
   - ☐ 1 (not well)

3. In the Vocabulary Builder, how many words did you match correctly with their definitions?
   - ☐ 3 (6–8 words)
   - ☐ 2 (3–5 words)
   - ☐ 1 (0–2 words)

4. How well were you able to identify the main idea sentences and supporting details in this article?
   - ☐ 3 (extremely well)
   - ☐ 2 (fairly well)
   - ☐ 1 (not well)

5. How well do you understand why this article is called "In the Tiger's Lair"?
   - ☐ 3 (extremely well)
   - ☐ 2 (fairly well)
   - ☐ 1 (not well)

Vocabulary Check

Look back at the work you did in the Vocabulary Builder. Then answer each question by circling the correct letter.

1. When a tiger runs off into the bamboo forest, it leaves heavy pug marks in the mud. What are pug marks?
   a. an animal's dead body
   b. paw prints
   c. a wild animal's home

2. Which vocabulary word means "quietly hunting"?
   a. pant
   b. prey
   c. stalking

3. Female tigers are pregnant with their young for 95 to 112 days. What is a period of pregnancy called?
   a. gestation
   b. carcass
   c. lair

4. A tiger's stripes help camouflage it. What does *camouflage* mean?
   a. The stripes help the tiger blend with its surroundings.
   b. The stripes make the tiger easy to see.
   c. The stripes help keep the tiger cool.

5. What does the word *pant* mean as it is used in this selection?
   a. a pair of trousers
   b. sweat heavily
   c. breathe heavily

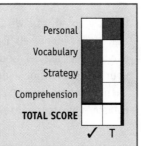

Add the numbers that you just checked to get your Personal Checklist score. Fill in your score here. Then turn to page 211 and transfer your score onto Graph 1.

Personal
Vocabulary
Strategy
Comprehension
TOTAL SCORE
✓ T

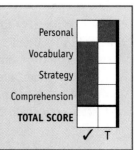

Check your answers with your teacher. Give yourself 1 point for each correct answer, and fill in your Vocabulary score here. Then turn to page 211 and transfer your score onto Graph 1.

Personal
Vocabulary
Strategy
Comprehension
TOTAL SCORE
✓ T

Strategy Check

Review the main idea table you completed in the Strategy Follow-up. Also review the selection if necessary. Then answer these questions:

1. How does the number of tigers in India in 1930 compare with the number today?
   a. In 1930, there were fewer than 2,000 tigers. Today there are about 40,000.
   b. In 1930, there were about 40,000 tigers. Today there are fewer than 2,000.
   c. In 1930, there were about 40,000 tigers. Today there are about the same number.

2. What happened to the tigers during World War II?
   a. Crowds of people followed tigers and shot them from jeeps.
   b. Packs of wild dogs attacked the tigers.
   c. People and animals stole their food.

3. Which of the following is *not* a way that tigers were killed by people?
   a. Poachers shot them.
   b. People fed them poisoned meats.
   c. People sprayed them with insecticide.

4. Suppose you created a main idea table for the paragraphs on where tigers live. Which of the following could you include as a supporting detail?
   a. Siberia, India, and China are three distant places where tigers live.
   b. Tigers of the southern jungles tend to be more brightly colored than those of the northern forests.
   c. The tiger hunts alone, wandering over a vast territory to find prey.

5. What main idea sentence would be supported by details about a tiger's attempt to stalk its prey?
   a. The tiger sleeps between feedings.
   b. A tiger works very hard for its food.
   c. After the kill, the tiger roars loudly.

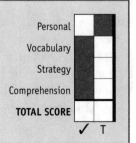

Check your answers with your teacher. Give yourself 1 point for each correct answer, and fill in your Strategy score here. Then turn to page 211 and transfer your score onto Graph 1.

Personal
Vocabulary
Strategy
Comprehension
TOTAL SCORE

Comprehension Check

Review the article if necessary. Then answer these questions:

1. Which of the following statements about a tiger's markings is true?
   a. The markings on one side of a tiger's body are the same as those on the other side.
   b. No two tigers have the same markings.
   c. Most tiger coats have light stripes and dark markings.

2. How does a tiger hunt?
   a. The tiger hunts alone, wandering over a vast territory to find its prey.
   b. Tigers hunt in groups.
   c. The tiger hunts alone, never wandering far from its lair.

3. How does a tiger usually kill a deer?
   a. by drowning it
   b. with a suffocating bite to the throat
   c. by snatching the animal out of a stream

4. How long do tiger cubs stay with their mothers?
   a. for two or three days
   b. for 95 to 112 days
   c. for two to three years

5. Who or what are the tiger's worst enemy?
   a. humans
   b. grazing animals
   c. wild boars

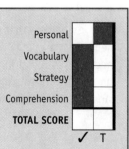

Check your answers with your teacher. Give yourself 1 point for each correct answer, and fill in your Comprehension score here. Then turn to page 211 and transfer your score onto Graph 1.

Personal
Vocabulary
Strategy
Comprehension
TOTAL SCORE

Extending

Choose one or both of these activities:

RESEARCH THREATS TO TIGERS

Tigers are an endangered species. Use the resources listed on this page to find out more about how tigers are threatened. Find out why tigers are endangered today and what's being done to save them. Share your findings with your classmates.

CREATE A "SAVE THE TIGER" POSTER

Using the resources listed on this page, create a "Save the Tiger" poster. Your poster should convince people that the tiger is an endangered species that's worth saving. Use paints, markers, or clippings from newspapers and magazines to create a colorful, eye-catching poster.

Resources

Books

Bailey, Jill. *Save the Tiger.* Save Our Species: Earth's Endangered Creatures. Steck-Vaughn, 1990.

Cajacob, Thomas. *Close to the Wild: Siberian Tigers in a Zoo.* Carolrhoda Nature Watch Book. Carolrhoda, 1985.

Harman, Amanda. *Tigers.* Endangered! Benchmark Books, 1996.

Web Sites

http://www.5tigers.org/Directory/kids.htm
Read about the five subspecies of tigers on this Web site. The site includes games and activities.

http://www.tigersincrisis.com/
This Web site contains photographs and videos of tigers and discusses the crisis that tigers face.

Multimedia Kit

Habitats: Realm of the Tiger Resource Kit. National Geographic Society, 1998.
This kit includes videos, picture pack, posters, and resources for teacher and student.

Learning New Words

VOCABULARY

From Lesson 12
- acquaintance
- assistance
- awkwardly
- consternation
- gravely
- logical
- pitiful
- sensitive

From Lesson 13
- indecent

Root Words

As you learned in Lesson 12, a root word is a complete word by itself. You can add prefixes and suffixes to a root word to make new words. For example, *trust* is a root word. You could add prefixes and suffixes to *trust* to make a variety of words with different meanings, such as *trusting, trustworthy, untrustworthy,* and *distrust.*

For each word below, find the root word and write it on the line.

1 disgraceful   _____

2. underachiever   _____

3. insufferable   _____

4. uneventful   _____

5. immeasurable   _____

Prefixes

A prefix is a word part that is added to the beginning of a root word. For example, the prefix *dis-* means "no" or "not," so adding *dis-* to the verb *agree* makes it *disagree,* a verb meaning "not agree."

in-

The prefix *in-* means "not." In "Elizabeth Blackwell, Pioneer Doctor" you learned that it was considered *indecent,* not decent, for a woman to work outside the home as a doctor. Notice that adding this prefix does not change the part of speech.

Now write the word that means the same as the phrases below.

1. not visible   _____

2. not effective   _____

3. not direct   _____

4. not active   _____

5. not expensive   _____

Suffixes

A suffix is a word part that is added to the end of a root word. When you add a suffix, you often change the root word's meaning and function. For example, the suffix *-ist* means "person or thing who studies _____," so adding the suffix *-ist* to the noun *behavior* makes it a noun meaning "a person who studies behavior."

-ly

The suffix *-ly* turns an adjective into an adverb that means "in a _____ manner or way." In "Jump for Center" you learned that although Pete worked *arduously* (in an arduous, or strenuous, manner) for three weeks, he was not picked to play center.

Draw a line from each word to its definition.

in a clumsy way	petulantly
in a bashful way	wonderfully
in a temperamental way	awkwardly
in a careful way	cautiously
in a remarkable way	shyly

-less

The suffix *-less* means "without." Adding it to a word changes it to an adjective. For example, adding *-less* to the word *thought* makes the adjective *thoughtless*, meaning "without thought."

Now write the definition of each phrase below.

1. without odor   _____

2. without time   _____

3. without taste   _____

4. without color   _____

5. without shoes   _____

The Day Grandfather Tickled a Tiger

Building Background

The story you are about to read has a surprise ending. A **surprise ending** is an unexpected twist at the end of a story's plot. The surprise may occur as a sudden change in the story's action or as an unexpected discovery. Think about a movie you've seen or a story you've read with a surprise ending. Was the twist in plot a change in action or an unexpected discovery? Were there any clues that might have helped you guess how the story would end? As you read "The Day Grandfather Tickled a Tiger," be aware of clues that might help you figure out its ending.

crouch

gleaming

reunion

scornful

shooed

slink

sly

stammered

Vocabulary Builder

1. The boldfaced words in the questions below are all from "The Day Grandfather Tickled a Tiger." Before you begin reading the story, underline the correct answer in as many of the questions as possible.

2. If you can't figure out some of the words, find them in the story, read them in context, and then try to figure them out. Then go back and answer the questions. See how many you can answer without using a dictionary.

3. Save your work. You will use it again in the Vocabulary Check.

    a. Would an animal in a **crouch** be standing on its hind legs, bending down low to the ground, or leaping high in the air?

    b. Does a **gleaming** car look shiny, dirty, or damaged?

    c. At a **reunion,** do you meet people for the first time, get back together with people you know, or say good-bye to people?

    d. If someone gave you a **scornful** look, would the person have a mocking expression, a frightened expression, or a confused expression?

    e. If you **shooed** someone, would you want the person to come closer, to go away, or to walk faster?

f. When animals **slink,** do they creep, run fast, or stand still?

g. If someone gave you a **sly** look, would the person look happy, surprised, or sneaky?

h. Is a **stammered** sentence spoken very clearly, spoken very loudly, or spoken very uncertainly?

Strategy Builder

Using Story Elements to Make Predictions

- In Lesson 11 you made predictions as you read the story "Damon and Pythias." As you know, a **prediction** is a kind of guess. When you make predictions, you base them on clues from the story. For example, you can base your predictions on events that have already happened in the story. Or you can base them on what you learn about the characters.

- In "The Day Grandfather Tickled a Tiger," there are two main characters: Grandfather and a tiger named Timothy. As you read this story, pay attention to the descriptions of these two characters. You might be able to base your predictions on the descriptions of their behavior and personalities.

The Day Grandfather Tickled a Tiger

By Ruskin Bond

Look for clues as you read to help you predict what might happen next. Pay particular attention to the descriptions of the characters' behavior and personalities. Also, look for clues that might help you figure out the story's surprise ending.

Timothy, our tiger cub, was found by my grandfather in a forest in northern India. Grandfather discovered the little tiger on a forest path hidden among the roots of a banyan tree. Grandfather took the beast home, where Grandmother gave him the name Timothy.

Timothy's favorite place in the house was the drawing room. He would settle himself comfortably on the sofa and would snarl only when anyone tried to make him get down. One of his favorite games was to stalk who- ever was playing with him. And so, when I went to live with Grandfather, I became one of the tiger's pets. With a **sly** look in his eyes and his body in a deep **crouch**, he would creep closer and closer to me. Suddenly he would make a dash for my feet. Then, rolling on his back and kicking with delight, he would make believe he was biting my ankles.

By this time he was the size of a full-grown golden retriever. When I took him for walks, people on the road would stay clear of us.

 Stop here for Strategy Break #1.

Strategy Break #1

1. What do you predict will happen next? _____
   _____
   _____

2. Why do you think so? _____
   _____
   _____

3. What clues from the story helped you make your prediction(s)? _____
   _____
   _____
   _____

➡ Go on reading to see what happens.

When Timothy was about six months old, his stalking became more dangerous, and he had to be chained up more often. Even the people in our house started to become afraid of him. When he started following the cook around the house, Grandfather decided it was time to give the animal to a zoo. The nearest zoo was at Lucknow, some two hundred miles away. I begged Grandfather to let me come along, for I would miss Timothy. So Grandfather bought a first-class compartment for the two of us and Timothy, and we set forth. When we arrived at the zoo, the people there were pleased to receive the tiger.

Grandfather and I had no chance to see how Timothy was doing at the zoo until about six months later. He and I went to the zoo and directly to Timothy's cage. The tiger was there, crouched in a corner. He was full-grown, his beautiful striped coat **gleaming** with health.

"Hello, Timothy," Grandfather said. I stayed outside the fence. But Grandfather climbed over the fence and put his arm through the bars of the cage. Timothy came over and allowed Grandfather to put both arms around his head. Grandfather stroked the big tiger's forehead and tickled his ears. Each time Timothy growled, Grandfather gave him a smack across the mouth. This had been Grandfather's way of keeping the animal quiet when Timothy had been living with us.

Timothy licked Grandfather's hand. Yet the tiger seemed upset, springing away when a leopard in the next cage snarled at him. But Grandfather **shooed** the leopard off, and Timothy returned to licking his hands. Every now and then the leopard would rush at the bars, and Timothy would again **slink** back to a far corner.

A number of people had gathered to watch the **reunion**. A keeper asked Grandfather what he was doing. "I'm talking to Timothy," said Grandfather. "Weren't you here when I gave him to the zoo six months ago?"

"I haven't been here very long," said the surprised keeper. "Please go on talking to the tiger. I have never been able to touch that tiger myself. He is very bad tempered."

 Stop here for Strategy Break #2.

Strategy Break #2

1. Do your earlier predictions match what happened? _____ Why or why not? _____
   _____
   _____

2. What do you predict will happen next? _____
   _____
   _____

3. Why do you think so? _____
   _____
   _____

4. What clues from the story helped you make your prediction(s)?_____
   _____
   _____

Go on reading to see what happens.

Grandfather had been stroking and slapping Timothy for about five minutes when he noticed another keeper. The keeper was looking at him with some alarm. Grandfather recognized him as the keeper who had been there when he had given Timothy to the zoo. "*You* remember me," said Grandfather. "Why don't you move Timothy to another cage, away from this dumb leopard?"

"But—sir," **stammered** the keeper, "it is not your tiger."

"I know that he is no longer mine," said Grandfather, a little angry. "But at least take my suggestion."

"I remember your tiger very well," said the keeper. "He died two months ago."

"Died!" cried Grandfather.

"Yes, sir, of pneumonia. This tiger was trapped in the hills only last month, and he is very dangerous!"

The tiger was still licking Grandfather's arm and enjoying it more all the time. Grandfather took his hand from the cage very slowly. With his face near the tiger's he said, "Good night, Timothy." Then, giving the keeper a **scornful** look, Grandfather took my hand, and we walked quickly out of the zoo. ●

Strategy Follow-up

Go back and look at all the predictions you wrote in this lesson. Do any of them match what actually happened in this story? Why or why not?

_____

_____

_____

_____

_____

_____

_____

_____

_____

_____

_____

_____

_____

_____

_____

_____

_____

✓Personal Checklist

Read each question and put a check (✓) in the correct box.

1. In Building Background, how well were you able to recall the surprise ending in a particular story or movie?
   - ☐ 3 (extremely well)
   - ☐ 2 (fairly well)
   - ☐ 1 (not well)

2. In the Vocabulary Builder, how many questions did you answer correctly and without using a dictionary?
   - ☐ 3 (6–8 questions)
   - ☐ 2 (3–5 questions)
   - ☐ 1 (0–2 questions)

3. How well do you understand why Grandfather gives Timothy to the zoo?
   - ☐ 3 (extremely well)
   - ☐ 2 (fairly well)
   - ☐ 1 (not well)

4. How well were you able to use clues in the story to figure out its surprise ending?
   - ☐ 3 (extremely well)
   - ☐ 2 (fairly well)
   - ☐ 1 (not well)

5. How well were you able to predict what would happen next in this story?
   - ☐ 3 (extremely well)
   - ☐ 2 (fairly well)
   - ☐ 1 (not well)

Vocabulary Check

Look back at the work you did in the Vocabulary Builder. Then answer each question by circling the correct letter.

1. When Grandfather leaves the zoo, he gives the keeper a scornful look. What does *scornful* mean?
   - a. mocking
   - b. frightened
   - c. confused

2. Which word best describes Timothy's behavior when the leopard rushes toward him?
   - a. shooed
   - b. crouch
   - c. slink

3. At the zoo, Timothy's coat is gleaming with health. What does *gleaming* mean?
   - a. dirty
   - b. shiny
   - c. damaged

4. Which word best describes the keeper's speech when he explains that the tiger in the zoo is not Grandfather's?
   - a. shooed
   - b. stammered
   - c. sly

5. A number of people watch the reunion between Grandfather and Timothy. What does *reunion* mean?
   - a. a getting back together
   - b. a saying good-bye
   - c. a first-time meeting

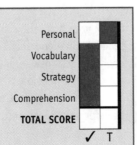

Add the numbers that you just checked to get your Personal Checklist score. Fill in your score here. Then turn to page 211 and transfer your score onto Graph 1.

Personal
Vocabulary
Strategy
Comprehension
TOTAL SCORE
✓ T

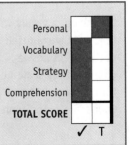

Check your answers with your teacher. Give yourself 1 point for each correct answer, and fill in your Vocabulary score here. Then turn to page 211 and transfer your score onto Graph 1.

Personal
Vocabulary
Strategy
Comprehension
TOTAL SCORE
✓ T

Strategy Check

Look back at what you wrote at each Strategy Break. Then answer these questions:

1. At Strategy Break #1, if you had predicted that Grandfather would have to give up Timothy, which clue would have best supported your prediction?

   a. Timothy's favorite place in the house was the drawing room.

   b. When I took him for walks, people on the road would stay clear of us.

   c. Suddenly he would make a dash for my feet.

2. Which clue suggests that Timothy fiercely guards his own territory?

   a. He would snarl when anyone tried to make him get down from the sofa.

   b. He would make believe he was biting the narrator's ankles.

   c. He would stalk whoever was playing with him.

3. At Strategy Break #2, which prediction would have best fit the story?

   a. The tiger in the cage will attack Grandfather.

   b. The tiger in the cage will attack the leopard.

   c. The tiger in the cage is not Timothy.

4. Which clue from the story suggests that the tiger is not Timothy?

   a. Yet the tiger seemed upset, springing away when a leopard in the next cage snarled at him.

   b. Timothy licked Grandfather's hand.

   c. Timothy came over and allowed Grandfather to put both arms around his head.

5. At Strategy Break #2, if you had predicted that the tiger would not hurt Grandfather, which clue would have best supported your prediction?

   a. The tiger kept licking Grandfather's hands.

   b. The tiger kept growling at Grandfather.

   c. The keeper said the tiger was bad tempered.

Comprehension Check

Review the story if necessary. Then answer these questions:

1. What was one of Timothy's favorite games when he was a cub?

   a. stalking people

   b. snarling at people

   c. sleeping on the sofa

2. Why did Grandfather give Timothy to the zoo?

   a. Grandfather wanted to sell the tiger.

   b. Timothy got very big, and his stalking became more dangerous.

   c. Grandfather was afraid of Timothy.

3. How does Grandfather treat the tiger at the zoo?

   a. He strokes the tiger and then slaps it when it growls at him.

   b. He stays outside the fence and doesn't touch the tiger.

   c. He ignores the tiger and pets the leopard.

4. What is the story's surprise ending?

   a. Timothy has become very bad tempered and dangerous.

   b. The tiger in the cage isn't Timothy.

   c. The tiger attacks Grandfather.

5. Why do you think Grandfather gives the keeper a scornful look as he walks out of the zoo?

   a. He is angry that the keeper placed a leopard beside the tiger.

   b. He and the keeper are old enemies.

   c. He is scornful because the keeper didn't tell him about the tiger sooner.

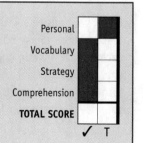

Check your answers with your teacher. Give yourself 1 point for each correct answer, and fill in your Strategy score here. Then turn to page 211 and transfer your score onto Graph 1.

Personal
Vocabulary
Strategy
Comprehension
TOTAL SCORE
✓ T

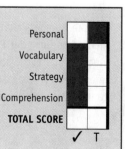

Check your answers with your teacher. Give yourself 1 point for each correct answer, and fill in your Comprehension score here. Then turn to page 211 and transfer your score onto Graph 1.

Personal
Vocabulary
Strategy
Comprehension
TOTAL SCORE
✓ T

Extending

Choose one or more of these activities:

ILLUSTRATE A SCENE

Illustrate a favorite scene from the story. Then ask your teacher if you can display the picture in the classroom.

WRITE A NEW ENDING

Write a new ending for "The Day Grandfather Tickled a Tiger." You might want to write a different surprise ending. Or you might want to write what would have happened if the tiger in the cage had been Timothy.

LEARN ABOUT ZOOS

With a partner, learn about zoos by visiting them and talking to the staff who work there. You can also use the resources listed on this page. Try to get answers to the following questions: How do zoos acquire animals? How are the animals treated? What's being done to improve their care? Share your findings with your classmates.

Resources

Books

Nirgiotis, Nicholas. *No More Dodos: How Zoos Help Endangered Wildlife.* Lerner, 1996.

Smith, Rolland. *Cats in the Zoo.* The New Zoo. Millbrook Press, 1994.

Web Sites

http://www.cattales.org
Click on "At the Zoo" and then go to "See the Cats." This Web page has photos of baby tigers being raised in captivity and updates about the babies.

http://www.wcs.org/kids
This Web site gives information on several zoos and on efforts to save wildlife.

The Midnight Visitor

Building Background

Ausable, the main character in "The Midnight Visitor," is a secret agent, or spy. Think about the spies you've encountered in other stories and movies. What characteristics do these spies have in common? How do they look and act? What kind of a world do they live in? Get together with a partner and talk about spies in fiction. Then, on the concept map below, list several words or phrases that describe the characteristics of a spy. Some examples are provided. When you have finished reading the story, compare the characteristics you listed with those displayed by Ausable. How does Ausable compare with other fictional spies?

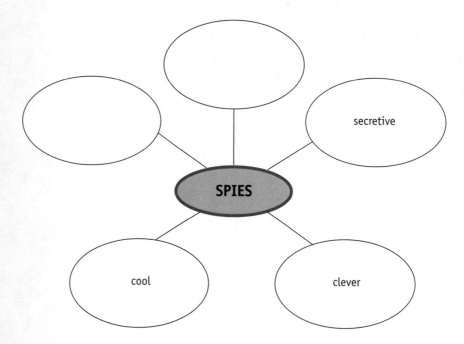

Vocabulary Builder

1. The words in the margin are from "The Midnight Visitor." On the clipboards, write a meaning for each word. (Use a dictionary, if necessary.) If a word has more than one meaning, predict how it might be used in the story and use that meaning.

2. Then use the vocabulary words and the title to help you predict what might happen in the story. Write your predictions on a separate sheet of paper. Use as many vocabulary words as possible.

3. Save your work. You will use it again in the Vocabulary Check.

authentic

automatic

disillusioned

espionage

gendarmes

grimly

menacing

mirth

Strategy Builder

Drawing Conclusions About Characters and Events

- Every story is told from a particular point of view. The **point of view** reveals the thoughts and feelings of the narrator—the one who is telling the story. "The Midnight Visitor" is told from a **third-person point of view**. That means that the narrator is not a character in the story. Instead, the narrator stands outside the story and relates all of the characters' actions. However, this type of narrator only tells as much as the author wants to reveal.

- As you read "The Midnight Visitor," think about what the narrator does and doesn't tell about the characters and events. Since the author doesn't tell you everything, you must draw your own conclusions about the characters and events.

- Remember that a **conclusion** is a decision you reach after thinking about information that the author gives you. You can base your conclusions on clues from the story, such as what a particular character says or does. You can also base your conclusions on what other characters say *to* or *about* that character.

CLIPBOARD

authentic

automatic

disillusioned

espionage

CLIPBOARD

gendarmes

grimly

menacing

mirth

The Midnight Visitor

By Robert Arthur

As you read the first part of this story, see what conclusions you can draw about the characters and events. Use what the characters say and do to help you draw your conclusions.

Ausable did not fit any description of a secret agent Fowler had ever read. Following him down the musty corridor of the gloomy French hotel where Ausable had a room, Fowler felt let down. It was a small room, on the sixth and top floor, and scarcely a setting for a figure of romantic adventure. But Ausable, in his wrinkled business suit badly in need of cleaning, could hardly be called a romantic figure.

He was, for one thing, fat. Very fat. And then there was his accent. Though he spoke French and German passably, he had never altogether lost the New England twang he had brought to Paris from Boston twenty years before.

"You are disappointed," Ausable said wheezily over his shoulder. "You were told that I was a secret agent, a spy, dealing in **espionage** and danger. You wished to meet me because you are a writer, young and romantic. You envisioned mysterious figures in the night, secret meetings, clever disguises.

"Instead, you have spent a dull evening in a French music hall with a sloppy fat man who, instead of having messages slipped into his hand by dark-eyed beauties, gets only a prosaic telephone call making an appointment in his room. You have been bored!"

The fat man chuckled to himself as he unlocked the door of his room and stood aside to let his discomfited guest enter.

"You are **disillusioned**," Ausable told him. "But take cheer, my young friend. Presently you will see a paper, a quite important paper for which several men have risked their lives, come to me in the next-to-the-last step of its journey into official hands. Some day soon that paper may well affect the course of history. In that thought there is drama, is there not?"

As he spoke, Ausable closed the door behind him. Then he switched on the light.

And as the light came on, Fowler had his first **authentic** thrill of the day. For halfway across the room, a small **automatic** in his hand, stood a man.

Ausable blinked a few times.

"Max," he wheezed, "you gave me a start. I thought you were in Berlin. What are you doing here in my room?"

Stop here for the Strategy Break.

Strategy Break

Use these questions to help you draw conclusions:

1. What does Fowler think of Ausable? _____

   _____

   _____

2. What does Ausable say about himself? _____

   _____

   _____

3. How does Ausable act when he discovers Max in his room? _____

   _____

   _____

4. What conclusions can you draw about Ausable so far? _____

   _____

   _____

➡ Go on reading to see what happens.

Max was slender, a little less than tall. His features suggested slightly the crafty pointed countenance of a fox. There was about him—aside from the gun—nothing especially **menacing**.

"The report," he murmured. "The report that is being brought you tonight. I thought it would be safer in my hands than in yours."

Ausable moved to an armchair and sat down heavily.

"I'm going to raise the devil with the management this time, and you can bet on it," he said **grimly**. "This is the second time in a month somebody has gotten into my room off that confounded balcony!"

Fowler's eyes went to the single window of the room. It was an ordinary window, against which now the night was pressing blackly.

"Balcony?" Max said, with a rising inflection. "No, a passkey. I did not know about the balcony. It might have saved me some trouble had I known."

"It's not my balcony," Ausable said with extreme irritation. "It belongs to the next apartment."

He glanced explanatorily at Fowler.

"You see," he said, "this room used to be part of a large unit, and the next room—through that door there—used to be the living room. *It* had the balcony, which extends under *my* window now.

"You can get onto it from the empty room two doors down—and somebody did, last month. The management promised me to block it off. But they haven't."

Max glanced at Fowler, who was standing stiffly a few feet from Ausable, and waved the gun with a commanding gesture.

"Please sit down," he suggested. "We have a wait of half an hour at least, I think."

"Thirty-one minutes," Ausable said moodily. "The appointment was for twelve-thirty. I wish I knew how you learned about that report, Max."

The other smiled without **mirth**.

"And we wish we knew how it was gotten this far," he replied. "However, no harm has been done. I will have it back—what is that?"

Unconsciously Fowler, who was still standing, had jumped at the sudden rapping on the door. Ausable yawned.

"The **gendarmes**," he said. "I thought that so important a paper as the one we are waiting for might well be given a little extra protection tonight."

Max bit his lip in uncertainty. The rapping was repeated.

"What will you do now, Max?" Ausable asked. "If I do not answer, they will enter anyway. The door is unlocked. And they will not hesitate to arrest you."

The man's face was pale as he backed swiftly toward the window; with his hand behind him he flung it up to its full height, and swung a leg over the sill.

"Send them away!" he rasped. "I will wait on the balcony. Send them away or I'll make you regret it!"

The rapping on the door became louder. And a voice was raised.

"M'sieu! M'sieu Ausable!"

Keeping his body twisted so that he could still watch the fat man and his guest, the man at the window grasped the frame with his free hand to support himself as he rested his weight on one thigh, then swung his other leg up and over the sill.

The doorknob turned. Swiftly Max pushed with his left hand to free himself from the sill and drop to the balcony outside. And then, as he dropped, he screamed once, shrilly.

The door opened and a waiter stood there with a tray, a bottle and two glasses.

"M'sieu, the beverage you ordered for when you returned," he said, and set the tray upon the table, deftly uncorked the bottle, and retired.

White-faced, Fowler stared after him.

"But—" he stammered, "the police—"

"There were no police," Ausable sighed. "Only Henri, whom I was expecting."

"But won't that man out on the balcony—" Fowler began.

"No," Ausable said, "he won't return. You see, my young friend, there is no balcony." ●

Strategy Follow-up

Use these questions to help you draw conclusions:

1. What seems to anger Ausable most about finding Max in his room? _____

_____

_____

2. Why do you think Ausable tells Max about the balcony?_____

_____

_____

3. Why does Ausable say that the gendarmes are at his door? _____

_____

_____

4. What do you think happens to Max? _____

_____

_____

5. What conclusion can you draw about Ausable's skill as a secret agent? _____

_____

_____

✓Personal Checklist

Read each question and put a check (✓) in the correct box.

1. At the beginning of the story, how well do you understand why Fowler is disillusioned?
   - ☐ 3 (extremely well)
   - ☐ 2 (fairly well)
   - ☐ 1 (not well)

2. How well were you able to use the vocabulary words to predict what might happen in the story?
   - ☐ 3 (extremely well)
   - ☐ 2 (fairly well)
   - ☐ 1 (not well)

3. How well were you able to draw conclusions about the story's characters and events?
   - ☐ 3 (extremely well)
   - ☐ 2 (fairly well)
   - ☐ 1 (not well)

4. In Building Background, you listed some of the characteristics of a spy. How well were you able to compare the characteristics you listed with those displayed by Ausable?
   - ☐ 3 (extremely well)
   - ☐ 2 (fairly well)
   - ☐ 1 (not well)

5. How well do you understand what happened to Ausable's midnight visitor?
   - ☐ 3 (extremely well)
   - ☐ 2 (fairly well)
   - ☐ 1 (not well)

Vocabulary Check

Look back at the work you did in the Vocabulary Builder. Then answer each question by circling the correct letter.

1. Which meaning of *automatic* is used in this story?
   a. mechanical
   b. car
   c. gun

2. Which of the following words refers to Ausable's profession?
   a. espionage
   b. gendarmes
   c. mirth

3. Which vocabulary word best describes Fowler's feeling as he walks to Ausable's hotel room?
   a. menacing
   b. disillusioned
   c. grimly

4. Which of the following might cause you to feel mirth?
   a. a joke
   b. a funeral
   c. a ghost story

5. Fowler feels his first authentic thrill when he sees Max in Ausable's room. What does *authentic* mean?
   a. real
   b. fearful
   c. excitement

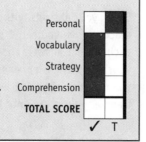

Add the numbers that you just checked to get your Personal Checklist score. Fill in your score here. Then turn to page 211 and transfer your score onto Graph 1.

Personal
Vocabulary
Strategy
Comprehension
TOTAL SCORE
✓ T

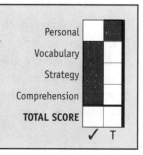

Check your answers with your teacher. Give yourself 1 point for each correct answer, and fill in your Vocabulary score here. Then turn to page 211 and transfer your score onto Graph 1.

Personal
Vocabulary
Strategy
Comprehension
TOTAL SCORE
✓ T

Strategy Check

Review what you wrote in the Strategy Break and Follow-up. Also review the rest of the story. Then answer these questions:

1. Why do you think Fowler feels let down when he first meets Ausable?
   a. Ausable doesn't look like the spies Fowler has probably seen in the movies.
   b. Ausable is exactly what Fowler expects.
   c. Ausable isn't a real spy.

2. Why does Ausable tell Max about the balcony outside of his room?
   a. He wants to trick Max.
   b. He believes that Max got into his room from the balcony.
   c. He wants Max to use the balcony to escape from the gendarmes.

3. What conclusion did you draw about what happens to Max?
   a. He falls to his death from Ausable's window.
   b. He gets away from the gendarmes.
   c. He is waiting on the balcony.

4. What conclusion did you draw about Ausable's skill as a spy?
   a. He makes a lot of careless mistakes.
   b. He doesn't know how to handle himself in dangerous situations.
   c. He's very clever and keeps calm in dangerous situations.

5. At the end of the story, what does Fowler probably think of Ausable?
   a. Fowler is still disappointed in Ausable.
   b. Fowler is frightened of Ausable.
   c. Fowler is very impressed with Ausable.

Comprehension Check

Review the story if necessary. Then answer these questions:

1. What does Ausable look like?
   a. He's well-dressed and handsome.
   b. He has the crafy pointed face of a fox.
   c. He's a fat man who wears wrinkled business suits.

2. Why has Max come to Ausable's room?
   a. He's a writer who wants to meet a real secret agent.
   b. He wants the report that is being delivered to Ausable.
   c. He comes to have a beverage with Ausable.

3. Why does Ausable really tell Max the story about the balcony?
   a. He's setting Max up.
   b. He makes up stories when he's nervous.
   c. He wants to find out if Max used the balcony.

4. What happens when someone knocks at the door?
   a. Max runs out of the door.
   b. Max jumps out of the window.
   c. Max starts shooting.

5. Who knocks at the door?
   a. the police
   b. Fowler
   c. Henri, a waiter

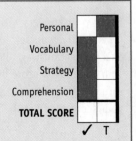

Check your answers with your teacher. Give yourself 1 point for each correct answer, and fill in your Strategy score here. Then turn to page 211 and transfer your score onto Graph 1.

Personal
Vocabulary
Strategy
Comprehension
TOTAL SCORE
✓ T

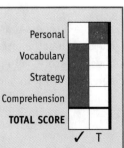

Check your answers with your teacher. Give yourself 1 point for each correct answer, and fill in your Comprehension score here. Then turn to page 211 and transfer your score onto Graph 1.

Personal
Vocabulary
Strategy
Comprehension
TOTAL SCORE
✓ T

Extending

Choose one or more of these activities:

LEARN ABOUT REAL SECRET AGENTS
Conduct research to find out more about the life and work of real secret agents. Begin your research with the resources listed on this page. Present your findings in an oral or written report.

REWRITE THE STORY
Get together with a small group of classmates and write the story from Fowler's point of view. Use first-person pronouns such as *I, me, my,* and *mine* to tell what Fowler is thinking when he sees Max in Ausable's room. Is he frightened? What does he feel when Max rushes toward the window? What does he say when Ausable tells him that there is no balcony?

PERFORM THE STORY
With a few other students, prepare a performance or a dramatic reading of "The Midnight Visitor." If possible, videotape or tape-record your performance. Otherwise, simply perform the story live before your class.

ILLUSTRATE A SCENE
Choose a scene from "The Midnight Visitor" to illustrate. For example, you might want to draw the scene in the hotel room when Ausable and Fowler discover Max hiding there. Or you might want to illustrate the scene when Max slips out of the window. Use the descriptions in the story to help you.

Resources

Books
Melton, H. Keith. *The Ultimate Spy Book.* Dorling Kindersley, 1996.

Platt, Richard. *Spy.* Eyewitness. DK Publishing, 2000.

Wiese, Jim. *Spy Science: 40 Secret-Sleuthing, Code-Cracking, Spy-Catching Activities for Kids.* Wiley, 1996.

Web Sites
http://www.fbi.gov/kids/6th12th/6th12th.htm
This is the youth page of the Federal Bureau of Investigation's Web site.

http://userpages.aug.com/captbarb/spies.html
This Web site has information about real women who were spies and secret agents.

The Crane Maiden

busily

frantically

instantly

joyfully

miraculously

readily

tenderly

CLIPBOARD

busily

root word: busy

in an active manner

frantically

root word:

instantly

root word:

joyfully

root word:

CLIPBOARD

miraculously

root word:

readily

root word:

tenderly

root word:

Building Background

The selection you are about to read is a Japanese folktale. In Lesson 12 you read "Arap Sang and the Crane," an African folktale. As you may recall, a folktale is a simple story that has been passed down from generation to generation. Folktales often have both humans and animals as main characters. They also can include supernatural elements—beings that couldn't exist or events that couldn't happen in the real world.

Think about the stories that are told in your family about you or other family members. Which one would you like to see passed down from generation to generation? Write a brief summary of the story on the lines below.

_____

_____

_____

_____

_____

_____

Vocabulary Builder

1. Each vocabulary word in the margin ends in the suffix *-ly*. A suffix is a word part that is added to the end of a word. When you add a suffix, you often change the word's meaning and function. For example, adding the suffix *-ly* to the root word *weak* changes the adjective *weak* to the adverb *weakly,* meaning "in a weak manner, or way."

2. For each word on the clipboards, write the root word. Notice that in some cases, the addition of the suffix changes the spelling of the root word. Then write what the word means with the suffix added. Use context clues from the story or a dictionary to help you figure out any unfamiliar words. The first one has been done for you.

3. Save your work. You will use it again in the Vocabulary Check.

Strategy Builder

Identifying Causes and Effects in Stories

- As you learned when you read "Lucky to Be Alive," many stories contain cause-and-effect relationships. Remember that a cause tells *why* something happened. An effect tells *what* happened. To find a cause-and-effect relationship while you read, ask yourself, "What happened?" and "Why did it happen?"

- As you read the following paragraph, think about what happens, and why.

> Because the day was fine, a man sat in his lawn chair, eating a sandwich. The man's cat crept under the lawn chair, tail twitching, when it saw a bird hopping through the low branches of a nearby tree. Suddenly, a crumb from the man's sandwich fell to the ground. Eyeing the tasty crumb, the bird hopped down from the tree to inspect it. In a flash, the unseen cat leaped out from underneath the chair, causing the terrified bird to screech and fly right at the man. Startled, the man jumped up from his chair and knocked it over. The chair fell onto the cat, who ran to the house for cover.

- If you wanted to track the causes and effects in this paragraph, you could put them on a **cause-and-effect chain**. It might look like this:

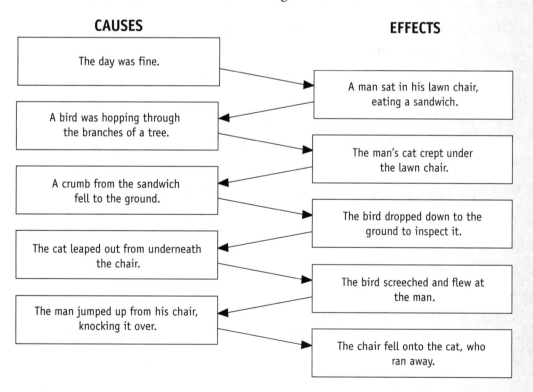

CAUSES	EFFECTS
The day was fine.	A man sat in his lawn chair, eating a sandwich.
A bird was hopping through the branches of a tree.	The man's cat crept under the lawn chair.
A crumb from the sandwich fell to the ground.	The bird dropped down to the ground to inspect it.
The cat leaped out from underneath the chair.	The bird screeched and flew at the man.
The man jumped up from his chair, knocking it over.	The chair fell onto the cat, who ran away.

The Crane Maiden

By Miyoko Matsutani

As you read the first part of this story, you can apply the strategies that you just learned. To find the causes and effects, keep asking yourself, "What happened?" and "Why did it happen?"

Long years ago, at the edge of a small mountain village in the snow country of Japan, there lived an old man and his wife. They had little in this world that they could call their own, but they were happy in their life together.

Now one winter morning the old man set out for the village with a bundle of firewood fastened to his back. It was bitter cold. He knew he would have little trouble selling the wood. Then with the money he would buy some food so that he and his wife could have a good supper.

As the old man trudged through the falling snow he was suddenly aware of a fluttering sound and a pitiful cry of *Koh, koh.* Turning from the path to investigate, he came upon a great crane **frantically** trying to free herself from a trap.

The old man's heart was touched with pity for the magnificent bird. While he tried to soothe the crane with tender words, his hands released the cruel spring of the trap. At once the crane flew up, **joyfully** calling *Koh, koh,* and disappeared into the snowy sky.

With a lighter step the old man went on through the snow. When he had sold his wood he returned once more to his humble house. As his old wife busied herself with preparing supper, he told her about rescuing the crane.

"That was a good deed," she said. "Surely you will one day be rewarded for your kind heart."

As she spoke these words there came a tapping on the door. The old wife hastened to see who was there. Upon opening the door she beheld a beautiful young girl standing in the swirling snow. Her delicate face glowed like a peach beginning to ripen in the summer sun. Her dark eyes sparkled in the dancing firelight from the hearth.

"Forgive my knocking at your door," she said in a soft voice. "I have lost my way in the snow. May I share the warmth of your fire tonight?" Then, bowing low before the two old people, she said, "My name is Tsuru-san."

"Oh, you poor child!" cried the old wife. "Come in at once before you freeze in the bitter cold." They sat the girl down close to the hearth, and the old wife piled more wood on the flames so that the girl would soon be warm.

The old couple shared their simple supper of hot porridge with Tsuru-san. Then they gave her their bed with its warm quilts to sleep on, while they spent the night huddled on a pile of straw.

In the morning when they awoke, the old man and his wife were surprised to see a good fire already burning on the hearth. The water urn was filled with fresh clear water. The floors had been swept. All the rooms were clean and tidy.

Tsuru-san, the sleeves of her kimono neatly tied back with a red cord, was **busily** stirring a pot over the fire. "Good morning," she said, bowing to the old couple. "If you will wash your hands we may eat breakfast. The porridge is cooked and ready."

"In our old age we have a daughter!" said the old man, laughing.

"We are being rewarded for your good deed of yesterday," replied his wife happily.

The snow and bitter cold continued for many days, and so Tsuru-san stayed in the shelter of the old couple's home. As she had neither mother nor father, it was at last decided that she would remain as a daughter to these people.

 Stop here for the Strategy Break.

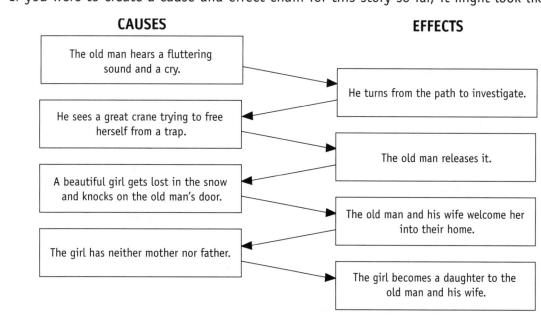

Strategy Break

If you were to create a cause-and-effect chain for this story so far, it might look like this:

CAUSES

- The old man hears a fluttering sound and a cry.
- He sees a great crane trying to free herself from a trap.
- A beautiful girl gets lost in the snow and knocks on the old man's door.
- The girl has neither mother nor father.

EFFECTS

- He turns from the path to investigate.
- The old man releases it.
- The old man and his wife welcome her into their home.
- The girl becomes a daughter to the old man and his wife.

Go on reading to see what happens.

The children of the neighborhood were soon attracted to the house because the girl was such a delight to be with. The house rang with happy laughter. The hearts of the old man and his wife were filled with joy at the sound.

And so the days of early winter passed. Soon it would be time for the great New Year celebration. The old man spoke to his wife, saying, "Tsuru-san has been such a delight to us. If only I could give her a gift of a new kimono."

"Or if I could make her a rice cake for the New Year," his wife added.

But the winter had been hard. The old man had not been able to cut wood to sell, so there was no money to buy even rice, much less a kimono.

Now Tsuru-san had overheard them talking. It grieved her that these good people should be so poor. Coming before them, she bowed low and said, "Dear parents, I know there has been no wood to sell. Perhaps I can help you and repay your great kindness to me. There is an old loom in the back room. I will weave cloth on it for you to sell in the village. Only you must promise that no one shall look at me while I am weaving."

The old man and his wife thought this was an odd request, but they **readily** agreed. Tsuru-san locked herself in the room. Soon they heard the sound of *Tin kola, kola, pon, pon, Tin kola, kola, pon, pon* as the shuttle sped back and forth and the fabric grew in length.

For three days this continued. Tsuru-san paused for neither food nor rest. Then at last the door opened and she stepped out, holding in her hands a bolt of cloth such as the old man and his wife had never seen in all their lives. They gasped at its beauty and marveled at its incredible softness.

"Dear father," said the girl, "take this cloth into the village and sell it. It will be but small payment for the happy home you have given me. Remember this, however," she continued, "do not put a price on this cloth, and you will fare better than you can imagine."

Without wasting a moment, the old man hurried into the center of the village. When people saw the beautiful cloth he was carrying, a crowd soon gathered.

"I will pay ten gold pieces for your cloth," said one man. "No, no!" cried another. "Sell it to me for twenty gold pieces!" "You would be a fool to sell it for such a price, old man," said another. "This is a bolt of rare twilled brocade. I will pay you fifty gold pieces for it." And so it went, with each man offering more, until the old man finally sold the cloth for one hundred pieces of gold.

Pausing only long enough to buy rice for rice cakes, a kimono for Tsuru-san, and a few delicacies for New Year's Day, the man hurried home with his pockets jingling. "Tomorrow, tomorrow is the New Year's Day," he sang. "The New Year is the happy time, eating rice cakes whiter than snow."

Then such a hustle and bustle there was, as the old man and his wife prepared for the feast. As he pounded the rice, his wife made it into fine white cakes. And on New Year's Day all the children came in for a great party with their friend Tsuru-san.

Still the cold days of winter followed one after the other. At last, one day Tsuru-san said to the old couple, "It is time for me to weave another bolt of cloth for you so that you will have money to live on until the spring returns. But remember what I told you. No one is to look at me while I am working."

Again they promised that they would not look, and the girl once more locked herself in the room and began weaving. *Tin kola, kola, pon, pon, Tin kola, kola, pon, pon* went the loom. One day passed, and then the second. Still the sound of the loom filled the house. By now, the neighbors had grown curious.

"Is Tsuru-san weaving again?" asked one.

"Ah, soon you will have more gold pieces to hide under the floor," said another, with a smile and a wink.

"The loom makes such an interesting sound," remarked the first one. "I would love to see what Tsuru-san is doing."

We have promised not to watch her while she works," said the old man.

"What an odd request," cried one of the people. "I would not make such a promise to *my* daughter, you can believe me. What harm could there be in taking one look?"

Now, in truth, the old woman had been most curious about Tsuru-san's weaving. Encouraged by her neighbor's remarks, she stepped up to a crack in the door.

"Stop, stop, old woman!" cried her husband when he saw what was happening. "Tsuru-san has forbidden it!" But it was too late. His wife had already peeked through the crack.

What a sight it was that met her eye! There, sitting at the loom, was a great white crane, pulling feathers from her body and **miraculously** weaving them into cloth.

The old woman stepped back from the door, and before she could relate what she had seen, the door opened. Out stepped Tsuru-san, thin and pale, holding in her hands a half-finished bolt of cloth.

"Dear parents," she said in a weak voice. "I am the crane you rescued from the trap. I wanted to repay your kindness by weaving you another bolt of cloth." Then her eyes filled with tears. "But now that you have seen me in my true form I can no longer stay with you."

With this she kissed the man and his wife **tenderly** and walked out of the house. **Instantly**, she became a crane once more. With a great whish of her wings she flew up into the sky. Slowly she circled overhead, then with a single cry of *Koh,* as if to say good-bye, the crane maiden was gone forever. ●

Strategy Follow-up

Complete this cause and effect chain for the second part of the story. Copy it onto another sheet of paper if you need more room to write. Some of the chain has been filled in for you.

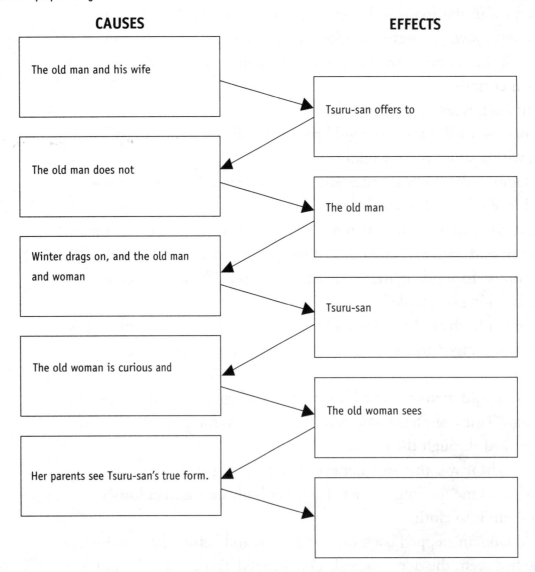

CAUSES

The old man and his wife

The old man does not

Winter drags on, and the old man and woman

The old woman is curious and

Her parents see Tsuru-san's true form.

EFFECTS

Tsuru-san offers to

The old man

Tsuru-san

The old woman sees

✓Personal Checklist

Read each question and put a check (✓) in the correct box.

1. How well did the activity in Building Background help you understand why stories are passed down in families and cultures?
   - ☐ 3 (extremely well)
   - ☐ 2 (fairly well)
   - ☐ 1 (not well)

2. In the Vocabulary Builder, how many words were you able to define correctly?
   - ☐ 3 (6–7 words)
   - ☐ 2 (3–5 words)
   - ☐ 1 (0–2 words)

3. How well were you able to identify the causes and effects in this story?
   - ☐ 3 (extremely well)
   - ☐ 2 (fairly well)
   - ☐ 1 (not well)

4. How well do you understand why Tsuru-san wants to help the old man and his wife?
   - ☐ 3 (extremely well)
   - ☐ 2 (fairly well)
   - ☐ 1 (not well)

5. How well do you understand why Tsuru-san leaves the old man and his wife?
   - ☐ 3 (extremely well)
   - ☐ 2 (fairly well)
   - ☐ 1 (not well)

Vocabulary Check

Look back at the work you did in the Vocabulary Builder. Then answer each question by circling the correct letter.

1. Which vocabulary word means "in a willing manner"?
   a. readily
   b. instantly
   c. tenderly

2. The crane frantically tries to free herself from a trap. What does *frantically* mean?
   a. in a joyful manner
   b. in a distressed manner
   c. in a gentle manner

3. Which vocabulary word has the opposite meaning of *busily*?
   a. happily
   b. actively
   c. lazily

4. Which vocabulary word means "in a wonderful manner"?
   a. miraculously
   b. joyfully
   c. instantly

5. After Tsuru-san kisses the man and his wife, she instantly becomes a crane. What does *instantly* mean?
   a. in an active manner
   b. in a happy manner
   c. in a quick manner

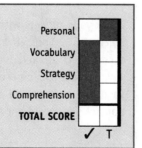

Add the numbers that you just checked to get your Personal Checklist score. Fill in your score here. Then turn to page 211 and transfer your score onto Graph 1.

Personal
Vocabulary
Strategy
Comprehension
TOTAL SCORE
✓ T

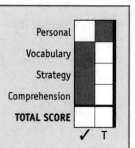

Check your answers with your teacher. Give yourself 1 point for each correct answer, and fill in your Vocabulary score here. Then turn to page 211 and transfer your score onto Graph 1.

Personal
Vocabulary
Strategy
Comprehension
TOTAL SCORE
✓ T

Strategy Check

Look back at the cause-and-effect chain that you completed for the second part of this story. Then answer these questions:

1. Why does Tsuru-san offer to weave cloth for the old man and his wife?
   a. because the wife needs a new kimono
   b. because they don't have enough money
   c. because the old man can no longer work

2. What is the effect when the old man does not put a price on the cloth?
   a. He sells it for 100 gold pieces.
   b. He sells it for 10 gold pieces.
   c. He sells it for 50 gold pieces.

3. What causes Tsuru-san to weave another bolt of cloth?
   a. The neighbors ask her to weave some more cloth.
   b. The old man and woman ask her to weave another bolt.
   c. Winter drags on, and the old man and woman need money until spring returns.

4. What causes the old woman to peek at Tsuru-san while her daughter is weaving?
   a. The old woman is curious.
   b. The old man tells her to look.
   c. Tsuru-san forbids her to look.

5. What is the effect when the old man and his wife see Tsuru-san's true form?
   a. Tsuru-san weaves them another bolt of cloth.
   b. Tsuru-san can no longer stay with them and flies away.
   c. Tsuru-san dies.

Comprehension Check

Review the story if necessary. Then answer these questions:

1. How does the old man's wife respond when he tells her about rescuing the crane?
   a. She is angry.
   b. She tells him he will be rewarded.
   c. She tells the neighbors.

2. Who knocks on the old couple's door on a bitterly cold night?
   a. the adults of the neighborhood
   b. the children of the neighborhood
   c. Tsuru-san

3. What does Tsuru-san overhear the old man and woman saying to each other?
   a. that they want to have a party and invite all the neighbors
   b. that they want to give Tsuru-san a kimono and a rice cake
   c. that they want Tsuru-san to weave cloth for them

4. Why does Tsuru-san make the old couple promise not to watch her weave?
   a. She doesn't want them to know that she is a crane.
   b. She is very shy and hates to be watched.
   c. She doesn't want them to learn her secrets as a weaver.

5. The second time Tsuru-san weaves, why does she only finish half a bolt of cloth?
   a. She grows weak from plucking her own feathers and cannot finish.
   b. She stops weaving as soon as the old woman breaks her promise.
   c. She runs out of feathers.

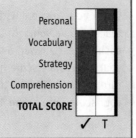

Check your answers with your teacher. Give yourself 1 point for each correct answer, and fill in your Strategy score here. Then turn to page 211 and transfer your score onto Graph 1.

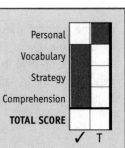

Check your answers with your teacher. Give yourself 1 point for each correct answer, and fill in your Comprehension score here. Then turn to page 211 and transfer your score onto Graph 1.

Extending

Choose one or more of these activities:

PERFORM THE FOLKTALE

Work with other students to create a puppet play, a skit, or a dramatic reading of "The Crane Maiden." Then share your performance with your class, a small group, or a younger class.

DRAW A KIMONO

In the story, the old man wants to buy Tsuru-san a beautiful kimono. Explore library or Internet resources (including those listed on this page) to find out more about kimonos. Then draw a picture of a kimono.

MAKE AN ORIGAMI CRANE

Origami is the traditional Japanese art of paper folding. Use the resource listed on this page to learn how to make an origami crane. Then talk to your teacher about setting up a display of the paper cranes in your classroom.

Resources

Books

Bang, Molly Garrett. *Dawn.* SeaStar, 2002.

Yagawa, Sumiko, and Katherine Paterson, trans. *The Crane Wife.* Morrow, 1987.

Yamanaka, Norio. *The Book of Kimono.* Kodansha International, 1987.

Web Sites

http://www.folds.net/tutorial/
This Web site provides instructions for origami, including how to make a paper crane.

http://www.japanesekimono.com
Learn about the kimono and other Japanese clothing on this Web site.

from First in the Field: Baseball Hero Jackie Robinson (Part 1)

Building Background

On April 15, 1947, Jackie Robinson became the first African American to play on a major-league team. In time, most people came to accept and admire Jackie. However, in the beginning, he had to endure almost overwhelming hatred and racism.

In breaking baseball's color barrier, Jackie did more than change baseball. He changed America. Today, athletes of all races compete on an equal basis in all sports. For his contribution to sports, Jackie Robinson's place in history is assured. But Jackie wanted to be remembered for just one thing—for being a great baseball player.

consolation

humiliation

impressionable

oppressive

perseverance

segregation

solace

Vocabulary Builder

1. Read the vocabulary words in the margin. If you do not know what any of the words mean, look them up in a dictionary.

2. Then circle the word or phrase in each row that is a synonym of the boldfaced vocabulary word.

consolation	comfort	communication	discouragement
humiliation	honor	award	shame
impressionable	sensitive	indifferent	in awe
oppressive	easy to bear	hard to bear	light to bear
perseverance	giving up	being different	being determined
segregation	uniting people	separating people	helping people
solace	relief	burden	sadness

Strategy Builder

How to Read a Biography

- In this lesson and Lesson 20, you will read excerpts from a biography of Jackie Robinson. As you may recall, a **biography** tells the story of a real person's life, and is written by someone else.

- The events in most biographies are told in the **sequence**, or time order, in which they happened. As you learned in Lesson 13, authors often use **signal words** to make that sequence as clear as possible. Remember that some signal words—such as *first, then,* and *later*—help you link one smaller event to the next in a biography. However, signal words such as *in 1919* or *seven years later* help you see the sequence of the major, or most important, events in a person's life.

- The paragraph below is from a biography of baseball player Roberto Clemente. Notice how the underlined signal words help you track the sequence of events in his life. (The words signaling major events are underlined twice.)

> Roberto Clemente was born in Puerto Rico <u>in 1934</u>. <u>When he was a boy</u>, he loved sports—especially baseball. <u>After playing amateur baseball</u>, Roberto signed with Montreal's Triple A team. <u>Then</u> he made the big time. He joined the Pittsburgh Pirates <u>in 1955</u>. Roberto played in two World Series and was chosen as the Most Valuable Player <u>in the 1971 series</u>. <u>Then</u> tragedy struck. <u>On December 31, 1972</u>, Roberto rode in a plane carrying supplies to earthquake-stricken Nicaragua. Unfortunately, the plane went down off the coast of Puerto Rico. <u>Just months after achieving 3,000 hits</u>, Roberto died.

- If you wanted to show the sequence of the major events described above, you could put them on a time line. It would look like this:

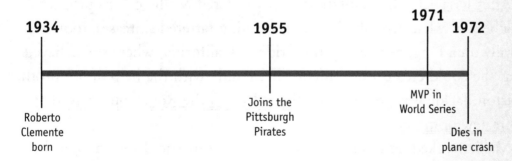

from First in the Field:
Baseball Hero Jackie Robinson (Part 1)

By Derek T. Dingle

Use what you've learned to track the events in Part 1 of Jackie Robinson's biography. Notice the underlined signal words as you read. They will help make the sequence clearer.

Jackie Robinson was born <u>in 1919</u> on the same plantation that his grandparents were forced to work as slaves before President Abraham Lincoln signed the Emancipation Proclamation in 1863. Although Jackie's parents were not in physical bondage, Mallie and Jerry Robinson—married since 1909—endured the hardship of being tenant farmers, toiling in the fields for a meager twelve dollars a month.

They were already having trouble making ends meet <u>when Jackie was born</u>. In addition to this new member of the family, they had to feed three growing young boys—Edgar, eleven; Frank, nine; Mack, seven—and one girl, five-year-old Willa Mae. But Mallie was determined to make life better for her clan, encouraging Jerry to negotiate with the plantation owner about making him a "half-cropper" so that instead of working for a pittance, he would receive half the profits from the crops produced. Even with the extra money, Jerry could not take the **oppressive** life of being a farmer, and he left Cairo, Georgia, to see what else the world had to offer, abandoning his thirty-year-old wife and five children.

<u>After Jerry left</u>, the plantation owner ordered Mallie off his property. Mallie sold what little she had and, carrying tattered suitcases, took her family on a long, exhausting train ride to California, where she believed that she could create a new life for her family with the help of her brother Burton. Jackie was <u>only six months old when the Robinsons arrived at their new home</u>.

Mallie worked hard, taking two jobs as a domestic. Even though she would get up before daylight to go to work and come home exhausted, she still spent time with the Robinson kids, preaching to them the importance of family unity, religion, education, and kindness to others. Her example demonstrated hard work and **perseverance**—two qualities that would stick with Jackie the rest of his life. <u>Within seven years</u>, she saved enough to move to 1212 Pepper Street in Pasadena, California. Because of the size of the modest, two-story home, the Robinson kids called it "The Castle."

 Stop here for the Strategy Break.

Strategy Break

If you were to show the main events described in this biography so far, your time line might look like this:

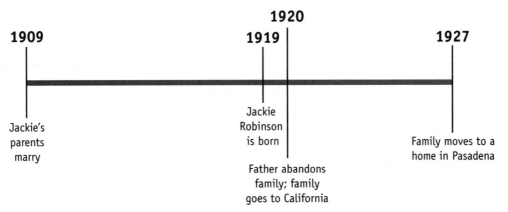

1909 — Jackie's parents marry

1919 — Jackie Robinson is born

1920 — Father abandons family; family goes to California

1927 — Family moves to a home in Pasadena

As you continue reading, keep paying attention to the order of events in Jackie's life. Use the signal words to help you. At the end of this selection, you will continue the time line on your own.

 Go on reading.

Times were still rough for the Robinson family at The Castle. Young Jackie and his family were the only African Americans living on the tree-lined block. They still did not have much money. Jackie often went to school hungry.

Young Jackie grew into a skilled player and a fierce competitor in every sport he played. He was so talented that his grade-school classmates would often bribe him to play on their team by offering part of their lunches or even a dollar. Jackie would take the money home and give it to his family.

He found a bit of **consolation** in sports. Even though he was applauded for his athletic skills, Jackie sometimes felt like an outsider. He was often teased and called names because of the color of his skin. He would ask himself, if everyone liked what he did on the playground so much, why did they treat him so badly?

Jackie sought **solace** at the movies, where he saw his other role model—besides his older brother Mack, by now a lightning-quick high-school track star—boxing legend Joe Louis.

The wiry, energetic Jackie and his pal "Little Jack" Gordon went to the local movie theater to see the big, brawny boxer, who was known as the "Brown Bomber" for his coffee-colored complexion and his explosive right hook. Because Jackie and Little Jack were black, they had to sit in a special section of the theater. Jackie forgot about that, though, sitting in the dark theater and watching the black-and-white image of Joe Louis clobbering yet another opponent in the ring. Jackie would swing his hands furiously, imitating the champ's every move. The two friends' viewing was often cut short when the usher would shoo them out of the theater for making too much of a racket. As Jackie made his way home, he would marvel at the rare sight of a black man competing as an equal with a white man and emerging a winner.

Despite the example of the Brown Bomber and the teachings of his mother, Jackie was frustrated by the twin demons of poverty and racism. Before the Civil Rights movement in the 1950s and 1960s, black people and other nonwhites often experienced **segregation** in more than theaters and restaurants. They could only play in the neighborhood YMCA one day a week and were only occasionally allowed to take a dip in the city's huge public swimming pool. Jackie sought out others who could relate to his experience. Unfortunately, Jackie fell in with the wrong crowd. He joined the Pepper Street Gang, a multicultural group of rebels who would stir up trouble throughout the neighborhood. The members of the rowdy gang were black, Mexican, and Japanese kids who lived a few blocks away from The Castle and, like Jackie, were treated as outcasts.

It was in the Pasadena of the late 1920s that Jackie suffered one of his greatest **humiliations**. Once Jackie and his friends were escorted to jail at gunpoint by the sheriff because they went for a swim in the local reservoir. Held and questioned under hot lights for hours by the sheriff and his deputies, Jackie and his friends suffered from heat exhaustion. They begged for something cold to drink or eat. The deputies brought Jackie and his friends watermelon and placed it on the floor. Eating off the floor, they consumed the watermelon to nourish their dehydrated bodies. The officers jeered and photographed the youths as they gulped down the fruit. It was a day that Jackie would not forget, a memory that fueled his bitterness—and determination to elevate his status.

Jackie became the leader of the pack. His gang was different than those of today. They did not carry knives or guns, but they did engage in all sorts of mischief. The gang would stop traffic by throwing rocks at cars and streetlights, or take revenge on a homeowner who called them names by putting thick, sticky tar on his lawn. Jackie's mother found out about the tar incident and confronted her youngest child. With his head bowed in shame, Jackie led his band of marauders back to the gooey patch to clean it up.

But Mallie Robinson's scolding did not stop his activities with the Pepper Street Gang. Jackie's salvation came through the church.

One bright Sunday morning, the Robinsons went to their house of worship, Scotts Methodist Church, to meet the new minister. As usual, Jackie was restless, shifting around on the wooden bench in the pews. He would much rather be outside playing ball or causing mischief than listening to another boring sermon. But the tall, redheaded Pastor Karl Downs was different. He was a young, energetic, and athletic minister who played basketball and softball. One day, Pastor Downs sought out the leader of the Pepper Street Gang at their favorite street corner. Pastor Downs told Jackie and the boys that he was organizing clubs and sports teams. He convinced the rowdies to give the church program a try. Jackie was so taken by the young minister that eventually he volunteered to be a Sunday school teacher in Downs's church.

Pastor Downs convinced the **impressionable** young Jackie to put his energy once again into sports. Now he could improve his athletic skills in a place where he would not be an outsider, in an organized church league. It did not take Jackie long to trade his gang membership for a team uniform. ●

Strategy Follow-up

Now continue the time line by filling in only the major events. Since the author does not say exactly when the events occurred, just be sure to list them in the right order. In Lesson 20, you will continue the time line as you read part 2 of Jackie Robinson's biography.

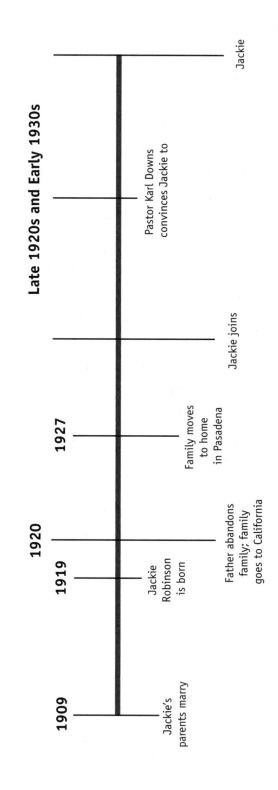

1909
Jackie's parents marry

1919
Jackie Robinson is born

1920
Father abandons family; family goes to California

1927
Family moves to home in Pasadena

Jackie joins

Late 1920s and Early 1930s
Pastor Karl Downs convinces Jackie to

Jackie

✓ Personal Checklist

Read each question and put a check (✓) in the correct box.

1. How well did the information in Building Background help you understand how Jackie Robinson changed America?
   - ☐ 3 (extremely well)
   - ☐ 2 (fairly well)
   - ☐ 1 (not well)

2. In the Vocabulary Builder, how many synonyms did you identify correctly?
   - ☐ 3 (6–7 synonyms)
   - ☐ 2 (3–5 synonyms)
   - ☐ 1 (0–2 synonyms)

3. How well do you understand why Mallie Robinson tried to teach Jackie the importance of hard work and perseverance?
   - ☐ 3 (extremely well)
   - ☐ 2 (fairly well)
   - ☐ 1 (not well)

4. How well do you understand why Jackie joined a gang?
   - ☐ 3 (extremely well)
   - ☐ 2 (fairly well)
   - ☐ 1 (not well)

5. In the Strategy Follow-up, how well were you able to organize the events of Jackie's life on the time line?
   - ☐ 3 (extremely well)
   - ☐ 2 (fairly well)
   - ☐ 1 (not well)

Vocabulary Check

Look back at the work you did in the Vocabulary Builder. Then answer each question by circling the correct letter.

1. Jackie Robinson was an impressionable young man. What does *impressionable* mean?
   - a. sensitive
   - b. indifferent
   - c. in awe

2. Which phrase is a synonym of *segregation*?
   - a. helping people
   - b. uniting people
   - c. separating people

3. Which pair of vocabulary words are synonyms?
   - a. *consolation* and *solace*
   - b. *humiliation* and *perseverance*
   - c. *impressionable* and *segregation*

4. Which of the following might cause you to feel humiliation?
   - a. going to a party
   - b. being laughed at
   - c. receiving an honor

5. Mallie Robinson demonstrated perseverance. What does *perseverance* mean?
   - a. determination
   - b. being different
   - c. giving up

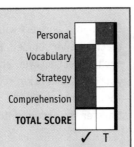

Add the numbers that you just checked to get your Personal Checklist score. Fill in your score here. Then turn to page 211 and transfer your score onto Graph 1.

Personal	
Vocabulary	
Strategy	
Comprehension	
TOTAL SCORE	✓ T

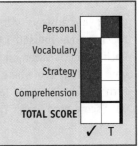

Check your answers with your teacher. Give yourself 1 point for each correct answer, and fill in your Vocabulary score here. Then turn to page 211 and transfer your score onto Graph 1.

Personal	
Vocabulary	
Strategy	
Comprehension	
TOTAL SCORE	✓ T

Strategy Check

Review the time line that you worked on in the Strategy Follow-up. Then answer these questions:

1. Which event happens before the Robinsons move to California?
   a. The family moves into a home in Pasadena.
   b. Jackie's father abandons the family.
   c. Jackie joins a gang.

2. According to the time line, what happened in 1909?
   a. Jackie's parents marry.
   b. Jackie is born.
   c. Jackie's family moves to California.

3. What does Pastor Karl Downs convince Jackie to do?
   a. throw rocks at cars
   b. join the Pepper Street gang
   c. join an organized church sports league

4. What happens after Jackie meets Pastor Karl Downs?
   a. He and his gang clean tar off a lawn.
   b. Jackie eats watermelon off the floor.
   c. Jackie trades his gang membership for a team uniform.

5. Which phrase is *not* an example of signal words?
   a. one day
   b. as usual
   c. in the late 1920s

Comprehension Check

Review the selection if necessary. Then answer these questions:

1. Why did the other grade-school kids tease Jackie?
   a. because he was black
   b. because of his athletic skills
   c. because he often went to school hungry

2. Besides his brother Mack, who was Jackie's hero?
   a. Pastor Karl Downs
   b. "Little Jack" Gordon
   c. Joe Louis

3. Why did Jackie join the Pepper Street gang?
   a. He wanted to join their sports league.
   b. He didn't want to join the YMCA.
   c. He wanted to be with other kids who were outcasts as a result of segregation.

4. Where did Jackie suffer his greatest humiliation?
   a. in a Pasadena jail
   b. in a Pasadena movie theater
   c. in a Pasadena school

5. What brought about Jackie's salvation?
   a. His mother scolded him and forced him to clean tar off of a lawn.
   b. Pastor Downs convinced him to give the church a try.
   c. The sheriff made him eat watermelon off the floor.

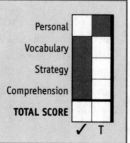

Check your answers with your teacher. Give yourself 1 point for each correct answer, and fill in your Strategy score here. Then turn to page 211 and transfer your score onto Graph 1.

Personal
Vocabulary
Strategy
Comprehension
TOTAL SCORE
✓ T

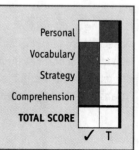

Check your answers with your teacher. Give yourself 1 point for each correct answer, and fill in your Comprehension score here. Then turn to page 211 and transfer your score onto Graph 1.

Personal
Vocabulary
Strategy
Comprehension
TOTAL SCORE
✓ T

Extending

Choose one or more of these activities:

LEARN ABOUT THE NEGRO LEAGUES

When Jackie Robinson was growing up, he dreamed about playing for the Negro leagues, the only teams at the time that African Americans could join. The Negro baseball leagues had such first-rate players as Satchel Paige and Josh Gibson. Use the resources listed on this page to learn more about the Negro leagues. Share your findings with your classmates.

SUMMARIZE THE SELECTION

Use the vocabulary words and your time line to summarize the events in Jackie's life. Try to use as many vocabulary words as possible in your summary. Also use signal words to help clarify the order of events. Then read your summary to a partner. Can he or she follow the order of events? Revise your summary as needed.

MAKE A BASEBALL CARD

Use the resources listed on this page to research Jackie's baseball career. Then make your own Jackie Robinson baseball card. Cut out a small piece of cardboard or poster paper. Glue Jackie's picture on one side of the card. On the other, write or type his statistics.

Resources

Books

McKissack, Patricia, and Fredrick McKissack Jr. *Black Diamond: The Story of the Negro Baseball Leagues.* Polaris, 1998.

Robinson, Jackie, and Alfred Duckett. *I Never Had It Made: An Autobiography of Jackie Robinson.* Ecco Press, 2003.

Santella, Andrew. *Jackie Robinson Breaks the Color Line.* Cornerstones of Freedom. Children's Book Press, 1996.

Web Site

http://sportsillustrated.cnn.com/baseball/mlb/all_time_stats/players/r/43112/
This Web site lists Jackie Robinson's career batting and base-running statistics.

http://www.blackbaseball.com
This Web site provides a history of the Negro baseball leagues.

from First in the Field:
Baseball Hero Jackie Robinson (Part 2)

Building Background

from **First in the Field (Part 1):**

One bright Sunday morning, the Robinsons went to their house of worship, Scotts Methodist Church, to meet the new minister. As usual, Jackie was restless, shifting around on the wooden bench in the pews. He would much rather be outside playing ball or causing mischief than listening to another boring sermon. But the tall, redheaded Pastor Karl Downs was different. He was a young, energetic, and athletic minister who played basketball and softball. One day, Pastor Downs sought out the leader of the Pepper Street Gang at their favorite street corner. Pastor Downs told Jackie and the boys that he was organizing clubs and sports teams. He convinced the rowdies to give the church program a try. Jackie was so taken by the young minister that eventually he volunteered to be a Sunday school teacher in Downs's church.

Pastor Downs convinced the impressionable young Jackie to put his energy once again into sports. Now he could improve his athletic skills in a place where he would not be an outsider, in an organized church league. It did not take Jackie long to trade his gang membership for a team uniform.

compete

dedicate

excelled

grieved

idolized

inspired

Vocabulary Builder

1. The vocabulary words in the margin are from *First in the Field,* Part 2. They describe some of the actions performed by Jackie Robinson and his brothers.

2. Read each of the following definitions. Then, on the line, write the action word that is being defined.

_____ a. greatly admired someone

_____ b. to commit yourself to a particular goal

_____ c. motivated to do something

_____ d. to strive to win

_____ e. felt great sadness

_____ f. did something extremely well

3. Save your work. You will use it again in the Vocabulary Check.

Strategy Builder

Reading a Biography

- In Lesson 19 you learned that a **biography** tells the story of a real person's life, and is written by someone else.

- As you discovered while reading Part 1 of Jackie Robinson's biography, the events in Jackie's life were told in the **sequence**, or time order, in which they happened. You used the **signal words** that the author provided to keep track of that sequence. Some of those signal words—such as *then, when,* and *one day*—helped you link one smaller event to the next. However, other signal words, such as *in 1919* or *seven years later,* helped you track the major events in Jackie's life.

- As you read Part 2 of Jackie Robinson's biography, keep using signal words to help you track the events in Jackie's life. Those signal words will help you as you continue the time line that you began in Lesson 19.

from First in the Field: Baseball Hero Jackie Robinson (Part 2)

by Derek T. Dingle

While the teachings of Pastor Downs helped turn him around, it was the athletic feats of his older brother Mack that **inspired** him. Jackie's muscular older brother **excelled** at basketball, baseball, and track and field, setting records in junior high school, high school, and college.

Mack was so good that he was picked to **compete** at the 1936 Olympics in Berlin, Germany. The bleary-eyed Robinson clan woke at 2 A.M. to hear the Olympics being broadcast from Germany. They huddled around the radio as the announcer called the finals of the 200-meter dash. All of the Robinsons cheered Mack as the young sprinter blasted from the starting blocks. "First out of the blocks is Mack Robinson. He is just flying. But here comes Jesse Owens. It's Robinson and Owens down to the wire. And it's Owens crossing the finish line."

The Robinson family fell silent. Jesse Owens would take Mack's place in history. Even so, Mallie said in hushed tones, "I am proud of my boy."

Jackie decided then and there that he would never finish second—in anything, or to anyone, including his brother Mack. In high school, he earned letters in basketball, football, track, and baseball. In basketball, he led his team in rebounding and scoring. He played running back and quarterback on the football field. In track-and-field events, he ran against—and beat—his older brother's records. But on the baseball field, he demonstrated his greatest skills: power hitting and stealing bases.

After high school, Jackie was ready to tackle his brother's records at Mack's alma mater—Pasadena Junior College. While attending college, Jackie finally shook the long shadow that his brother cast.

 Stop here for the Strategy Break.

Strategy Break

Now continue the time line that you began in Lesson 19. First, copy the time line below onto a long sheet of paper. Then add the major events from the part of Jackie's biography that you just read. Leave room at the end of your time line. You will finish it in the Strategy Follow-up.

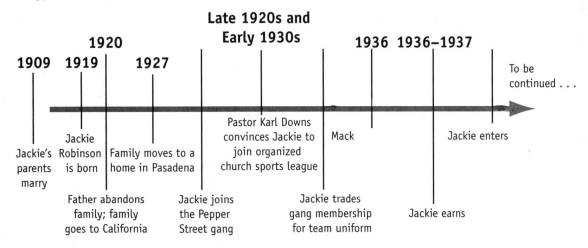

As you read the rest of this biography, continue to track the events in Jackie Robinson's life. Use the signal words to help you. When you get to the Strategy Follow-up, you will finish the time line.

 Go on reading.

One warm spring day, Jackie competed in two different events in two different cities. In the morning, Jackie traveled to Claremont, California, for a track-and-field event with his friend Johnny Burke. Less than a half hour away, the tire on their car blew out.

"I can't believe it. We're never going to make the meet," said Jackie. He was worried that if he showed up late, he wouldn't be allowed to compete.

"What's wrong, boys?" said the driver of a passing car. Jackie was in luck. It was the dean of his college. The dean offered his spare tire, which fortunately fit. Jackie and his friend left behind a trail of dust as they sped to the track meet. Jackie arrived just as his event—the broad jump competition—began, but he had no time to warm up. On his last of three attempts the lean, muscular athlete jumped 25 feet, 6 ½ inches, setting a new junior college national record for the broad jump—the record formerly held by Mack.

Jackie could not believe that he had broken his idol's record. But he had no time to pat himself on the back. He made a mad dash to a waiting car and headed to Glendale, California, for the state junior college baseball championship. Arriving mid-game, Jackie belted two hits and stole a base, helping his team win the championship. He was named the Most Valuable Junior College Player in Southern California in 1938.

Whenever Jackie made a special achievement in sports, he was always inspired by Mack's example. Unfortunately, he was always reminded that he had to rise above racism. Even though Mack was a great athlete with an Olympic medal, the only job that he could get was that of a street sweeper.

Despite the depressing reality, the spirit of the strapping young college star was boosted whenever he heard the cries "Go, Jackie, Go" from his own personal cheering section—his brother Frank. Although Jackie **idolized** Mack, he felt closest to Frank. Frank would often tell him, "Whatever happens, I'll be there for you, little brother."

One night in 1938, Jackie was at a neighbor's house playing cards when the phone rang. Frank, he learned, had been in a motorcycle accident. At the hospital, he could see the pain that was etched on Frank's face. His mother was crying. Jackie **grieved** for his brother that night, and the next morning, Frank died. Jackie would never forget Frank and would **dedicate** himself to excelling in sports as a way of honoring his dead brother.

That's just what Jackie did when he attended UCLA for two years, becoming the university's first "four-letter" man, establishing records in football, baseball, track, and basketball. Because of his athletic ability, Jackie left UCLA not only as a hero but a sports legend. ●

Strategy Follow-up

Now finish the time line that you began at the Strategy Break. The information below will help you.

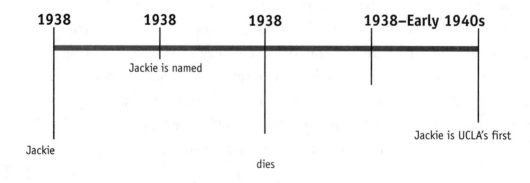

✓Personal Checklist

Read each question and put a check (✓) in the correct box.

1. You read in Building Background that Jackie Robinson left his gang to join a church sports team. How well do you understand why that decision was an important turning point in Jackie's life?
   - ☐ 3 (extremely well)
   - ☐ 2 (fairly well)
   - ☐ 1 (not well)

2. In the Vocabulary Builder, how many words did you define correctly?
   - ☐ 3 (5–6 words)
   - ☐ 2 (3–4 words)
   - ☐ 1 (0–2 words)

3. How well do you understand why Jackie idolized his brother Mack?
   - ☐ 3 (extremely well)
   - ☐ 2 (fairly well)
   - ☐ 1 (not well)

4. How well do you understand why Jackie decided he would never come in second in anything?
   - ☐ 3 (extremely well)
   - ☐ 2 (fairly well)
   - ☐ 1 (not well)

5. How well were you able to complete the time lines in the Strategy Break and Follow-up?
   - ☐ 3 (extremely well)
   - ☐ 2 (fairly well)
   - ☐ 1 (not well)

Vocabulary Check

Look back at the work you did in the Vocabulary Builder. Then answer each question by circling the correct letter.

1. Jackie grieved when Frank died. What does *grieved* mean?
   - a. did something extremely well
   - b. strove to win
   - c. felt great sadness

2. Which vocabulary word means "commit yourself to a particular goal"?
   - a. idolize
   - b. dedicate
   - c. compete

3. Which word best completes this sentence: "Jackie _____ when he broke his brother's broad jump record"?
   - a. excelled
   - b. idolized
   - c. competed

4. Jackie idolized Mack. What does *idolized* mean?
   - a. greatly admired someone
   - b. motivated to do something
   - c. did something extremely well

5. Which word best completes this sentence: "In one day, Jackie wanted to _____ in two different sporting events"?
   - a. compete
   - b. dedicate
   - c. inspire

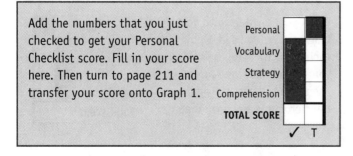

Add the numbers that you just checked to get your Personal Checklist score. Fill in your score here. Then turn to page 211 and transfer your score onto Graph 1.

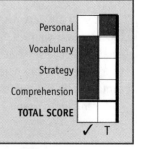

Check your answers with your teacher. Give yourself 1 point for each correct answer, and fill in your Vocabulary score here. Then turn to page 211 and transfer your score onto Graph 1.

Strategy Check

Review the time lines that you worked on in this lesson. Then answer these questions:

1. Which event happened in 1936?
   a. Frank dies.
   b. Jackie is named Most Valuable Junior College Player in Southern California.
   c. Mack competes in the Olympics.

2. Which event did *not* happen in 1938?
   a. Jackie earns letters in four high school sports.
   b. Frank dies.
   c. Jackie competes in two different sporting events.

3. Which event happened right after Frank died?
   a. Jackie becomes UCLA's first "four-letter" man.
   b. Jackie is named Most Valuable Junior College Player.
   c. Jackie enters UCLA.

4. Where did Jackie go after he finished high school?
   a. 1936 Olympics
   b. Pasadena Junior College
   c. UCLA

5. Where was Jackie a four-letter athlete?
   a. both in high school and at UCLA
   b. in high school only
   c. at UCLA only

Comprehension Check

Review the selection if necessary. Then answer these questions:

1. Who won the 200-meter dash at the 1936 Olympics in Berlin?
   a. Mack Robinson
   b. Jesse Owens
   c. Jackie Robinson

2. Why was Jackie determined to never take second place to anyone?
   a. He wanted to take his own place in history.
   b. He wanted to embarrass Mack.
   c. He wanted to make his mother proud.

3. What were Jackie's greatest athletic skills?
   a. power hitting and stealing bases on the baseball field
   b. playing running back and quarterback on the football field
   c. taking part in track-and-field events

4. Mack could only find work as a street sweeper. What did Mack's situation teach Jackie?
   a. that he shouldn't take part in the Olympics
   b. that he should stay in school
   c. that he had to rise above racism

5. How did Jackie decide to honor his dead brother?
   a. by going to UCLA
   b. by excelling in sports
   c. by becoming a street sweeper

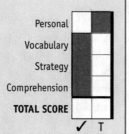

Check your answers with your teacher. Give yourself 1 point for each correct answer, and fill in your Strategy score here. Then turn to page 211 and transfer your score onto Graph 1.

Personal
Vocabulary
Strategy
Comprehension
TOTAL SCORE
✓ T

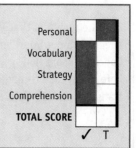

Check your answers with your teacher. Give yourself 1 point for each correct answer, and fill in your Comprehension score here. Then turn to page 211 and transfer your score onto Graph 1.

Personal
Vocabulary
Strategy
Comprehension
TOTAL SCORE
✓ T

Extending

Choose one or more of these activities:

LEARN ABOUT JESSE OWENS
Use some of the resources listed on this page to learn about Jesse Owens. In particular, answer this question: Why did his win at the 1936 Olympics anger Adolf Hitler, the German dictator who hosted the Games?

READ THE REST OF JACKIE'S BIOGRAPHY
Read the rest of Jackie Robinson's biography. Then create a time line that shows the major events in his life after he left UCLA.

DRAW JACKIE IN ACTION
Draw a picture of Jackie Robinson playing sports. You might show him playing baseball or running a track event in college. Or you might draw a picture of Jackie as a major-league baseball player. If you'd like, use the resources listed on this page to find sample pictures of Jackie.

Resources

Books
Ames, Lee J. *Draw 50 Athletes.* Main Street Books, 1989.

Denenberg, Barry. *Stealing Home: The Story of Jackie Robinson.* Scholastic, 1997.

Dingle, Derek T. *First in the Field: Baseball Hero Jackie Robinson.* Disney Press, 1998.

Sabin, Francene. *Jesse Owens, Olympic Hero.* Troll, 1997.

Web Sites
http://www.chron.com/content/chronicle/sports/special/barriers/index.html
This Web site contains information on the contributions that black athletes, including Jackie Robinson and Jesse Owens, have made to sports.

http://www.jackierobinson.com/about/photos/index.html
This Web site presents a photo gallery of images of Jackie Robinson.

Learning New Words

Root Words

A root word is a complete word by itself. You can add prefixes, suffixes, and other words to root words to make new words. For example, *trust* is a root word. You could add prefixes, suffixes, and other words to *trust* to make a variety of words with different meanings, such as *trusting, trustworthy, untrustworthy,* and *distrust.*

Choose a root word from Row 1, then combine it with a suffix from Row 2 and/or a prefix from Row 3 to make a word. Write the word and its definition on the lines below. If you don't know the definition of a word, look it up in the dictionary.

Row 1:	read	write	think	do	give
Row 2:	-able	-er			
Row 3:	re-	un-			

_____

_____

_____

_____

_____

_____

Foreign Words

The United States is made up of immigrants from many different countries. People brought their languages with them when they came here, and some words became part of American English.

In Lesson 17, "The Midnight Visitor," you encountered the word *espionage,* a French word that English has borrowed. Through context, you figured out that *espionage* means "spying." Use context to figure out the correct meaning of each underlined foreign word on page 209. Circle the letter of the correct meaning.

1. When she was five years old, Emily went to <u>kindergarten</u>.

   a. a garden for children

   b. school before first grade

2. The people who discovered gold in California yelled "<u>Eureka</u>!"

   a. I found it.

   b. Where is it?

3. In Hawaii, people often say "<u>Aloha</u>" when they arrive.

   a. Hello.

   b. How are you?

4. On party invitations, <u>R.S.V.P.</u> stands for *repondez s'il vous plait*.

   a. Tell the host if you are coming to the party.

   b. Ask the host if you can bring a friend.

Synonyms

A synonym is a word that has the same meaning as another word. The two words are the same part of speech, and can be used interchangeably. In Lesson 19 the author tells us that Jackie Robinson found a bit of *consolation* in sports. He could also have said that Jackie Robinson found a bit of *solace* in sports. By using a synonym of *consolation*, the sentences would have the same meaning.

Draw a line from the words in Column 1 to their synonyms in Column 2.

Column 1	Column 2
old	joyful
large	ill
loud	broad
wide	ancient
happy	noisy
sick	enormous

VOCABULARY

From Lesson 19
- consolation/ solace

Graphing Your Progress

The graphs on page 211 will help you track your progress as you work through this book. Follow these directions to fill in the graphs:

Graph 1

1. Start by looking across the top of the graph for the number of the lesson you just finished.

2. In the first column for that lesson, write your Personal Checklist score in both the top and bottom boxes. (Notice the places where *13* is filled in on the sample.)

3. In the second column for that lesson, fill in your scores for the Vocabulary, Strategy, and Comprehension Checks.

4. Add the three scores, and write their total in the box above the letter *T*. (The *T* stands for "Total." The ✔ stands for "Personal Checklist.")

5. Compare your scores. Does your Personal Checklist score match or come close to your total scores for that lesson? Why or why not?

Graph 2

1. Again, start by looking across the top of the graph for the number of the lesson you just finished.

2. In the first column for that lesson, shade the number of squares that match your Personal Checklist score.

3. In the second column for that lesson, shade the number of squares that match your total score.

4. As you fill in this graph, you will be able to check your progress across the book. You'll be able to see your strengths and areas of improvement. You'll also be able to see areas where you might need a little extra help. You and your teacher can discuss ways to work on those areas.

Graph 1

For each lesson, enter the scores from your Personal Checklist and your Vocabulary, Strategy, and Comprehension Checks. Total your scores and then compare them. Does your Personal Checklist score match or come close to your total scores for that lesson? Why or why not?
   Go down to Graph 2 and shade your scores for the lesson you just completed.

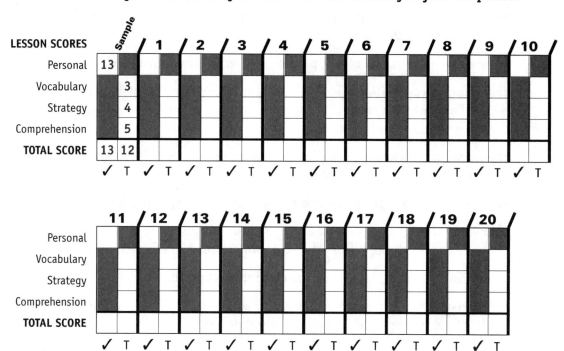

Graph 2

Now record your overall progress. In the first column for the lesson you just completed, shade the number of squares that match your Personal Checklist score. In the second column for that lesson, shade the number of squares that match your total score. As you fill in this graph, you will be able to check your progress across the book.

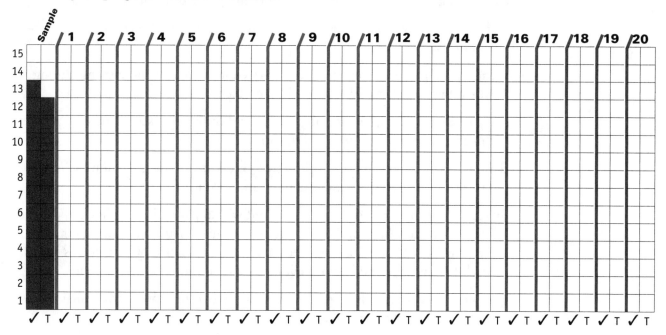

Glossary of Terms

This glossary includes definitions for important terms introduced in this book.

antonym   a word that means the opposite of another word. *Fast* and *slow* are antonyms of each other.

biography   the true story of a person's life, written by someone else.

cause-and-effect relationship   the relationship between events in a piece of writing. The cause in a cause-and-effect relationship tells *why* something happened; the effect tells *what* happened.

cause-and-effect chain   a graphic organizer used for recording the cause-and-effect relationships in a piece of writing.

characters   the people or animals that perform the action in a story.

character wheel   a graphic organizer used for recording the changes that a character goes through from the beginning to the end of a story.

comparing   looking at how two or more things are alike.

comparison chart   a graphic organizer used for showing how two or more people, places, things, or events are alike and different.

concept map   a graphic organizer used for recording the main ideas and supporting details in a piece of writing.

conclusion   a decision that is reached after thinking about certain facts or information.

conflict   problem faced by the main character.

context   information that comes before and after a word or situation to help you understand it.

contrasting   looking at how two or more things are different.

end result   the solution a character or characters try that finally solves the problem in a story.

event   a happening. The plot of any story contains one or more events during which the characters try to solve their problems.

features chart   a graphic organizer used for showing how several people, places, things, or events are alike and different.

fiction   stories about made-up characters or events. Forms of fiction include short stories, historical fiction, fantasy, and folktales.

folktale   a simple story that is usually told within particular families and cultures. Folktales usually have people and animals as main characters and supernatural elements. They also remind readers about the past, tell about a culture's values, teach lessons about human behavior, and are meant to be entertaining.

graphic organizer   a chart, graph, or drawing used to show how the main ideas in a piece of writing are organized and related.

headings   the short titles given throughout a piece of nonfiction. The headings often state the main ideas of a selection.

historical fiction   a made-up story based on real historical facts or events.

idiom   an expression that can't be understood by figuring out the meanings of the individual words.

informational article   a piece of writing that gives facts and details about a particular subject, or topic.

legend   a story that has been passed down from generation to generation. Legends are not true, but they are usually based on real people or events.

main idea   the most important idea of a paragraph, section, or whole piece of writing.

main idea table   a graphic organizer used for recording the main ideas and supporting details in a piece of writing.

main idea sentence   the sentence that tells what a paragraph, section, or whole piece of writing is about. The rest of the paragraph, section, or piece contains supporting details that tell more about the main idea.

multiple-meaning word   a word that has more than one meaning. The word *glare* is a multiple-meaning word whose meanings include "a very bright light," "a bright, smooth surface," and "an angry stare."

narrator the person or character who is telling a story.

nonfiction   writing that gives facts and information about real people, events, and topics. Informational articles and biographies are some forms of nonfiction.

outline   a framework for organizing the most important ideas in a piece of writing. Some outlines are organized according to a system of Roman numerals (I, II, III, IV, V, and so on) and capital letters (A, B, C, D, E, and so on).

plot   the sequence of events in a piece of writing.

point of view   the perspective, or viewpoint, from which a story is told.

prediction   a kind of guess that is based on the context clues given in a story.

prefix   a word part that is added to the beginning of a word.

problem   difficulty or question that a character must solve or answer.

problem-solution frame   a graphic organizer used for recording the problem, solutions, and end result in a piece of writing.

resolution   solution of the problem in a story.

root word   a complete word by itself. Other words or word parts can be added to root words to make new words.

sequence   the order of events in a piece of writing. The sequence shows what happens or what to do first, second, and so on.

sequence chain   a graphic organizer used for recording the sequence of events in a piece of writing. Sequence chains are used mostly for shorter periods of time, and time lines are used mostly for longer periods of time.

setting   the time and place in which a story happens.

signal words   words and phrases that tell when something happens or when to do something. Examples of signal words are *first, next, then, finally, after lunch,* and *two years later.*

solution   the things that characters or people do to solve a problem.

specialized vocabulary   words that are related to a particular subject, or topic. Specialized vocabulary words in the selection "How Buildings Take Shape" include *architect, horizontal,* and *truss.*

story map   a graphic organizer used for recording the main parts of a story: its title, setting, character, problem, events, and solution.

suffix   a word part that is added to the end of a word. Adding a suffix usually changes the word's meaning and function. For example, the suffix *-less* means "without," so the word *painless* changes the noun *pain* to an adjective meaning "without pain."

supernatural elements   beings that couldn't exist and/or events that couldn't happen in the real world.

supporting details   details that describe or explain the main idea of a paragraph, section, or whole piece of text.

surprise ending   an unexpected twist at the end of a story's plot.

synonym   a word that has the same meaning as another word. *Fast* and *quick* are synonyms of each other.

third-person omniscient point of view   point of view told by a narrator who is not a character in the story. The narrator stands outside the story and relates all of the characters' actions. However, this type of narrator tells only as much as the author wants to reveal.

time line   a graphic organizer used for recording the sequence of events in a piece of writing. Time lines are used mostly for longer periods of time, and sequence chains are used mostly for shorter periods of time.

title   the name of a piece of writing.

topic   the subject of a piece of writing. The topic is what the selection is all about.

Acknowledgments

Acknowledgment is gratefully made to the following publishers, authors, and agents for permission to reprint these works. Every effort has been made to determine copyright owners. In the case of any omissions, the Publisher will be pleased to make suitable acknowledgments in future editions.

"Arap Sang and the Cranes" from *Tales Told near a Crocodile* by Humphrey Harman. Copyright © 1967 by Humphrey Harman. Reprinted by permission of Curtis Brown, Ltd.

"Charlie Johnson" by Joe Smith. Reprinted by permisson of *Cricket* magazine, December 1998, Vol. 26, No. 4. Copyright © 1998 by Joseph K. Smith.

"The Crane Maiden" by Miyoko Matsutani, adapted from *The Crain Maiden.* Scholastic, Inc., 1968.

"Damon and Pythias: A Greek Legend" adapted by Teresa Bateman. Reprinted by permission of *Cricket* magazine, January 1999, Vol. 26, No. 5. Copyright © 1999 by Teresa Bateman.

"Dancing the Cotton-Eyed Joe" by Joann Mazzio. Reprinted by permission of *Cricket* magazine, March 1994, Vol. 21, No. 7. Copyright © 1994 by Joann Mazzio.

"The Day Grandfather Tickled a Tiger" by Ruskin Bond as appeared in *The National Observer,* 1965, Dow Jones & Company, Inc. Reprinted by permission of the author.

Elizabeth Blackwell, Pioneer Doctor by Matthew G. Grant. Copyright © 1974 Creative Education, 123 Broad Street, Mankato, MN 56001. Reprinted by permission.

"Fire!" by Caroline Evans from the October 1995 issue of *Ranger Rick* magazine, with the permission of the publisher, the National Wildlife Federation. Copyright 1995 by the National Wildlife Federation.

"The Fitting-In of Kwan Su" by Janet Gonter, as appeared in *Hopscotch*, Vol. 10, No. 2, August/September 1998. Reprinted by permission of the author.

"How Buildings Take Shape" by Kim Williams from *Highlights for Children,* March 1997, Vol. 52, No. 3, Issue 545. Copyright © 1997 by Highlights for Children, Inc., Columbus, Ohio. Reprinted by permission.

"In the Tiger's Lair" from *Lion Prides and Tiger Tracks* by Don Arthur Torgersen. Copyright © 1982 by Regensteiner Publishing Enterprises, Inc. Used by permission of the publisher.

"Jump for Center" by Barbara O. Webb in *Instructor*, March 1976. Copyright © 1976 by Scholastic Inc. Reprinted by permission.

"Just One of the Guys" by Donna Gamache as appeared in *Cricket*, December 1996, Vol. 24, No. 4. Copyright © 1996 by Donna R. Gamache. Reprinted by permission.

"The Lighthouse Keeper's Daughter" by Laura A. Badami. Reprinted by permission of *Cricket* magazine, January 1998, Vol. 25, No. 5. Copyright © 1998 by Laura A. Badami.